STUART MCHARDY is a writer
teller. Having been actively i
culture throughout his adult l
folklore – he has been residen
century. Although he has held some illustrious positions including
Director of the Scots Language Resource Centre in Perth and
President of the Pictish Arts Society, McHardy is probably proudest
of having been a member of the Vigil for a Scottish Parliament.
Often to be found in the bookshops, libraries and tea-rooms of
Edinburgh, he lives near the city centre with the lovely (and ever-
tolerant) Sandra and they have one son, Roderick.

Scotland's Future History

STUART McHARDY

Luath Press Limited
EDINBURGH
www.luath.co.uk

First published 2015
Reprinted 2015
Reprinted 2016
Reprinted 2017

ISBN: 978-1-910021-41-5

The paper used in this book is recyclable. It is made from
low chlorine pulps produced in a low energy, low emissions manner
from renewable forests.

Printed and bound by
Bell & Bain Ltd., Glasgow

Typeset in 10.5 point Sabon
by 3btype.com

for my son, Roderick

Contents

Foreword by Ian McHardy,
Hebridean Archaeologist

LET US BE CLEAR: the past does not dictate the future, or even the present. Let us not wallow in the past, using it to excuse our present day shortcomings, to blame others for those shortcomings, or to justify anti-English prejudice.

Let us not claim that the sun shines out of our own backsides, that we have clean karma sheets, or that Scotland's history is simply one of being unfairly beaten by our evil twisted neighbours.

Let us not claim the suffering of the common people in the Highland Clearances was any worse than that of most other native peoples throughout the world at the hands of similar foes.

Let us not claim that we were blameless in the genocidal colonialism which swept the world after those Clearances. Becoming the foe to so many other native peoples, after having been subject to such treatment in the first place, is possibly even more morally repugnant – we should have known better.

But above all, let us not feel sorry for ourselves with history. Doing so negates the potential of who we are and who we could be. I'm sure 'nature' hates a whinger as much as she loves a trier.

However, these 'whinges' are just some of the ways in which the past can, if not dictate, certainly help to shape identity in the present moment and actions in the future. This is as true in a personal sense as it is in the cultural or national: many talented individuals have been hamstrung by a lack of confidence, rooted in some painful childhood experience. Deep down they know they can do better, but success is just not happening. This could leave them with what can be called a 'Chip on the Shoulder'.

Scotland has often been seen as an appendage attached to the main body of activity down south (i.e. England). In terms of factors like political influence, people per square mile and global finance, this is perhaps an accurate depiction of Scotland today. However that backwater situation is not the way things always were, nor indeed the way things always need to be. So-called 'diffusionist' archaeologists of early 20th-century Britain such as V. Gordon Childe interpreted all the evidence in terms of waves of people or ideas coming from the south. This school of thought has been significantly challenged by archaeological discoveries indicating that, for example, the highly sophisticated Iron Age (c. 700BC – 700AD) Brochs (or Atlantic Round Towers, to give them their technical name) of northern Britain were actually invented in northern Britain and not copied from the south of England. A similar argument can be made today regarding Neolithic (4000BC – 2000BC) monuments – it seems the date, scale and sophistication of the monument at Ness of Brodgar in Orkney is such that the assumption of southern superiority or primacy must be questioned – especially if we look in terms of the whole of western Europe. The extreme west and north of the Atlantic coast seems to be where all the action was back then. Central Europe, Brussels for example, lacked any massive communal stone monuments at the time. As did London.

Thus History – and Archaeology – can create 'centres' and 'peripheries'. Much worse than that, there is no doubt that both have been used by Totalitarian and Colonial powers to legitimise their subjugation of people and even justify horrific ends. In North America, it was 'Manifest Destiny' that the Native people were killed and driven out of their land. In the 20th century, Adolf Hitler created the idea of a 'perfect' past of only Aryan people in order to justify forcibly creating that idea in the present. To offer a Scottish example particularly relevant to this book, James I of Scotland forcefully banned Gaelic from all Schools and Bibles and he sent the children of Chiefs and Lairds to be educated in the far south, force-feeding them a different view of life and the past, and pretty much starting the clearance of the common people.

As Jared Diamond argues in his book *Guns, Germs and Steel* (1997), there are reasons why some cultures overrun others, mostly to do with guns, germs and steel. However this was clearly not the case between Scotland and England as we both had all of the above. The reasons why should probably never be discussed under influence of alcohol, but suffice to say that in the end, most of today's government went to Eton.

In *Scotland's Future History*, Stuart McHardy describes some less dramatic, more insidious mechanisms which he argues have distorted our views of history without us barely noticing. One of the first things I agreed with Stuart about was that deep down in the unconscious of the south-centric perspective is the idea that the Romans were great – the best thing since sliced bread. Generations of scholars, historians, antiquarians, and let's face it, mostly toffs, have fawned and gushed over how bloody great the Romans were and what a shame it was they left. I find this bizarre. If the Romans were around today we would be calling them Nazis and spending every last drop of effort in fighting them to the death. We had our own indigenous culture and ways of life, admittedly not as advanced in terms of technology and organisation but arguably far superior in terms of ethics. Who knows what sort of society may have developed if these indigenous ways of life had been left to flourish. Our sycophantic worship of Romans may have, in turn, subconsciously justified our own subsequent British Empire and the atrocities carried out under its name, such as the genocide of Native Americans, Slavery of African people, and subjugation of countless others.

It is not a competition in sophistication which matters to me. That kind of competition has been constantly written about elsewhere. I care more that many peoples and ways of life have been lost, all over the world, crushed under the rumbling leviathan of War and Empire.

However, it may be argued that much has also resulted from

this, not least from the mixtures of different peoples thrown together in adverse situations and becoming friends. There's the rub: mixing isn't negotiable, it's essential. Even if you live on St Kilda. It all depends upon how it is done and it should be damned good fun! An equal footing for each person or culture would seem like the obvious place to start.

This is what Stuart is trying to achieve with this book – to redress the balance. If you accept the argument that history has been written by the winners, our history will contain many distortions. By going back and questioning some commonly, or nationally, held histories, we can have a profound effect upon important relationships today.

The Establishment may put this book down, criticise it for a supposed lack of sufficient scholarship, shakily supported conclusions or language unfit for a scholarly journal. This is because Stuart is not Establishment – he is a storyteller, a folklorist as well as a historian. By definition, he has grown from the grass roots.

Preface

There is a subject called British history, but so far as I can discover it consists of English history, with an occasional side-glance at Scotland at times when Scotland crossed England's path.

This is a society devoted to the study and furtherance of Scottish history, and it seems a little odd to me that this educational policy should still prevail. It is well calculated to condition the Scottish mind into turning instinctively towards London with the submission of the Moslem turning towards Mecca.

LORD COOPER, Lord President of the Court of Session, to the Scottish History Society 1948

IN THE PAST HALF CENTURY, Scotland has undergone a cultural resurgence. This, in turn, has helped develop current political trends where the possibility of the break-up of the United Kingdom is being treated as a distinct, possibly even likely, outcome. In this cultural resurgence, the indigenous languages of Gaelic and Scots, deliberately removed from the education system in the 1870s, have begun to re-assert themselves as the first languages of a substantial part of the Scottish population. There has also been a growing interest in Scotland's past as the Highland Clearances became studied and other periods like the 1st millennium and the 18th century have been given much more attention than formerly. Recently the stunning archaeological discoveries at Ness of Brodgar in Orkney have led to a fundamental questioning of what has traditionally been understood as Scotland's past. The investigation which started in 2002 has to date uncovered a wide range of artefacts and a series of structures, the most stunning of which is the Neolithic 'temple' known as Structure Ten. Dating from before 3000BCE with its five-metre thick walls, this is the largest Neolithic non-funerary stone structure ever found in Britain, long predating Stonehenge and the building of the pyramids in Egypt. The site was in use for over a thousand years and evidence suggests Structure Ten was replaced by eight smaller, similar but non uniform stone buildings. This may indicate a ritual site where separate groups, or tribes had their own sacred space. The investigation is ongoing and it is clear that there is more, and earlier material to be uncovered concerning what has been referred to as 'a Stone Age Cathedral'. This book argues that, in these and other areas, the actualities of Scotland's history have been neglected due to a perceived need within the political and educational establishments to present a version of our past that conforms wherever possible to the idea of Britishness that has been developed since the Union of 1707.

With the institution of the Scottish Parliament and the subsequent election to power of a party whose focus has been on Scotland – rather than the at-best nebulous notion of a Great Britain, which has lost 'the Great' – one very important result has been the official introduction of Scottish history into Scottish schools. It is an ongoing shame on the heads of succeeding generations of politicians and educators that this has had to be done – no other nation in Europe would countenance the possibility of not teaching their children about their own history and culture, yet we have had generations of such scandalous and servile behaviour. With the introduction of Scottish history into the official curriculum, however, we have to ask, what history? What should Scotland's Future History be? I suggest that it should be a history that is based on sound scholarship, but a scholarship that is rooted in a critical and even sceptical approach to interpreting the past. It is no coincidence that regime change throughout the world over millennia has often been accompanied by deliberate attempts to efface the story of the past and create a new one, in keeping with the beliefs of those coming into power. While we have never seen anything here quite as soul-numbing as the wanton destruction of the Buddhas of Bamiyan by the Taliban in 2001, Scottish history has been constantly and insidiously arranged to fit what can be interpreted as an essentially colonialist mentality. It is this issue that requires a sceptic's eye to ensure that we truly seek to have the best possible understanding of Scotland's history to pass on to succeeding generations. Anyone who writes history is working to an agenda, explicit or implicit, and to deny this is to fly in the face of common sense. To hope for a truly objective history developing in Scotland's future is perhaps to aim too high but we can hope to instil the idea that history must be subjected to substantial critique as an essential part of the process, not just of writing, but understanding, history. The concept of treating history forensically which is mentioned herein, would subject history to just the kind of examination that courts of law demand.

At the absolute centre of future Scottish history should be one simple idea. That we use what we know of ourselves to find out more. To this end I have already suggested in *A New History of the Picts* (2010), that we might well develop a better understanding of 1st-millennium Scotland by concentrating on the fact that the people then lived in tribal societies and use what we know of later clan and family histories in the Highlands and the Borders to help us gain a clearer understanding. Essentially Scotland's history should be what we, the Scots, no matter how recent, tell as our own story based on what we know and can discover about our predecessors here in Scotland itself. For far too long we have used the reality of so much of our early documentation having been destroyed, as an excuse to accept ideas of history that developed elsewhere as the core of our attempts to understand ourselves. The ongoing, and somewhat pathetic, fascination with the Romans in Scotland is a case in point, a fascination emanating

The excavations at the Ness of Brodgar

from our universities, funded directly from London, a city which, like the country in which it sits, was under Roman control for four centuries. Rightly the educational institutions of England are deeply interested in the Romans, since they helped to make the English people who they are. Their relevance in Scotland, while important, is not of the same order, but you would hardly know that from our history books.

Similarly we have had a story foisted on us that the last Jacobite rebellion was a Highland adventure by a flawed if Romantic young charmer that ended on Drummossie Moor, on 16 April 1746. This is simply not true and increasingly scholars are taking notice of the undoubted nationalist components of 18th-century Jacobitism in Scotland. We need a truer picture of our past than we have been given until now. In the future, it is absolutely necessary that we deal with the limitations of history as it has been taught thus far and hand on an approach to history that is critical, watchful and ever ready to change when evidence suggests it should.

As the Ness of Brodgar dig has shown, new evidence means new thinking. The very idea that around 10,000 people gathered in Orkney 5,000 years ago for a feast, apparently to celebrate the changing use of monumental stone-built buildings long before the Pyramids or Stonehenge were thought of, means we must begin to recalibrate the far past. I hope this selection of essays shows that we must recalibrate much more than that if we are to pass on the best, and most critically created picture of Scotland's past that we can to the coming generations.

Stuart McHardy
Edinburgh, 2015

Introduction

ALL MY LIFE I have had people ask me why I am so obsessed with Scotland's past. The word 'obsessed' hints that there is something a bit strange in my behaviour. Those asking me rarely thought of themselves as dyed-in-the-wool reactionaries – more often than not they thought of themselves as socialists. Of a sort. If anyone had suggested to them that an Inuit, a Native American, a Zimbabwean, a Høng or a Catalan was strange in trying to understand their own history and culture, my interrogators would have been appalled. Yet the idea that I should be so interested in finding out who I am and where I came from historically, gave them some feeling of unease. On pointing this out, I would be met with blustering generalities about having to stand together with the working class in England. Yet they would not have thought of telling a French or a German person to neglect their own history to concentrate on working with the workers of a neighbouring land. It was as if they could not understand what internationalism actually meant when it came to Scotland, as if we should deny our own cultural and historical identity. Those not of a left-leaning attitude have tended to move towards the argument that we live in the modern world and by caring too much about what was, after all, only one constituent part of a once mighty empire, I was turning my back on that modern world and all the material advances it represented. Move On; Get Over Yourself; History Belongs in The Past, etc.

This type of thinking is, of course, grounded in the delusive notion of perpetual progress, where economic development is seen as a form of Darwinian evolution in which material and technological advancement will endlessly continue 'to make things better'. Leaving aside the matter of for whom things have been getting better, the mounting evidence of global warming, accelerating depletion of natural resources and its consequent increasing habitat destruction tells us that that the grand idea of perpetual progress is a busted flush. The human race is facing ever harder times (though many of us have never had it easy at all) and the capitalist obsession with short-term return – the religion of Mammon, which most governments worldwide slavishly follow today – can only ensure that the rich scoop up more and more of the planet's limited resources to try and defend their established positions of privilege. Although I am not religious, I do appreciate the spiritual aspects of existence. Willie Shakespeare got it spot on when he wrote 'There are more things in heaven and earth than are dreamt of in thy philosophy, Jimmy'. The past is a different country, as the cliché says, but it is a country for which we have no map. Part of the problem of modern Western history, predicated on that spurious notion of eternal progress, is that all too often people of the past have been seen like foreigners denied the 'benefits' of European civilisation, as essentially cruder, more stupid and more primitive than we are, and thus essentially unenlightened. Perhaps the apogee of such thinking came from the pen of Lord Macaulay when he wrote, for the British Parliament, in *A Minute on Education* (1835):

> I am quite ready to take the oriental learning at the valuation of the orientalists themselves. I have never found one among them who could deny that a single shelf of a good European library was worth the whole native literature of India and Arabia.[1]

Hopefully many of us now know better than to dismiss other cultures, simply because they are different. Not all of us have moved on, however. In a world where recently in America insults have been thrown that people are using 'fact-based arguments', we can surely see how dangerous blinkered thinking can be.

The idea that those who do not learn from the mistakes of the past are bound to repeat them is self-evidently true.

After a lifetime of reading, debating, lecturing and writing on my country's past, I have come to the conclusion that far too much of what is presented as the history of my native land has been distorted, suppressed or ignored. It is not that it does not make sense. It is that it makes a sinister kind of sense. What has become obvious to me, as to many others, is that what is created as history for general consumption under the overall title of 'British history' is a deliberate fabrication intended to hide the realities of Scottish history. Why? Because the reality of Scottish history is simply that it is not English history. British history is English history with a few sops to the 'peripheral nations' thrown in. Thus we have a situation where the wars fought by Wallace and Bruce are referred to as the Scottish Wars of Independence. It cannot be stated too loudly or too often: Scotland was a nation state before England and was never part of England. It still isn't. So how in the name o some big hoose could we have ever fought a War of Scottish Independence? The details of that will be discussed later, but suffice to say this is a blatant example of how our history has been traduced. It has been going on for so long that people don't even notice it. When people believe a lie, the truth is invisible. The role of British history has been to legitimise the relatively recent political Union, which was pushed through against the wishes of the majority of Scots and was foisted upon us through corruption. Burns put it rather succinctly in 'A Parcel of Rogues in a Nation' (1791):

> What force or guile could not subdue
> Though many warlike ages
> Is wrought now by a traitor few
> For hireling traitors' wages.

That 'traitor few' have been followed by generations of native-born Scots happy to continue taking their pieces of silver and to maintain their own privilege by ensuring that our education system has avoided dealing with the realities of who we are and where we come from; happy to see themselves as part of a bigger gang. With our own parliament in place, it is time that we dealt with the reality that our history has been distorted for political reasons, and to ensure that future generations have a truer idea of their own history, whether or not the Scots decide to go it alone. It is time to move past the propaganda requirements of a British state whose ruling elite cling desperately to any trappings of their Imperial past, an Imperial past in which the Scots' place was all too often seen in a similar fashion to that of General Wolfe at the Heights of Abraham, when told that the Highland regiments were taking dreadful casualties, said 'It is no great mischief if they fall'.

This book is a series of essays on different aspects, and periods, of Scotland's past, that will hopefully open up debate. By exposing the extent of the distortion and suppression of Scottish history, I hope not to make too many value judgements. All history is speculative and no historian writes without a clear idea of what they want the reader to think. Whether this makes all history propaganda is a moot point, but all I can do is present what I think are the realities that need considering and ask you to think about them. It is important to realise that ideas can change – mine certainly have. My original impression of Prince Charles Edward Stuart was utterly unfavourable. I still believe him to have been a spoiled, arrogant and foolhardy young man (an occupational hazard of princes, it would seem), but what I have learned from looking closer at contemporary sources is that he was also charismatic, courageous and tough. That he had little or no interest in Scotland other than as a launching pad to fulfil his ambition of regaining the British throne for his father does not change that.

Knowledge also changes. The recent discoveries at Ness of

Brodgar in Orkney are having a profound effect on the understanding of prehistoric Britain, and the role of what we think of
as Scotland, the ramifications of which it will be interesting to see
unfold.[2]

The ideas in this book are entirely my own and I am as guilty
of bias as anyone else who attempts to interpret the past. I cannot
be other than who I am, just as Christian scribes of the 1st millennium could not help but be who they were. I can empathise with
them, even as I suggest that the stories they told of the world were
not the reality that I perceive it to have been. Trying to make sense
of the past involves considerable speculation and, of course, interpretation, particularly of the written word. Although two of the
essays here look at prehistoric times, the main thrust of the book
covers periods that are historical (i.e. periods from which we have
documents to help us understand what was happening). A fellow
member of the Pictish Arts Society, the late Sheriff of Forfar,
Stuart Kermack, made a point at a conference many years ago
about historical evidence. He suggested we should treat it forensically. By that he meant subject it to the same sort of rigorous
examination that is demanded in a court of law. This means that
nothing can be taken at face value – the motivation for the creation of all documentary evidence has to be considered. When the
Christian scribes developed from simple annal entries to writing
down 'history', their loyalty to their faith, and to the hierarchy of
their church, did not disappear. Their mindset was central to what
they wrote, just as much as Macaulay's was when he wrote his
well-regarded histories in the 19th century, and as mine is today.
Histories change as the world changes and what was obvious and
acceptable to Macaulay is seen by most of us as blinkered, ignorant and offensive. In time, this book may be seen in the same
way, and admittedly that time may even be now, for some. I
acknowledge that I have a bias towards looking for communal
ideas and beliefs as underpinning much of history, but I do try to

consider other opinions. What I will say is that, until very recently, history was simply about important men. That is, men deemed important by the people writing about them. Human society is much more complex than such a restricted viewpoint can ever appreciate, or properly interpret. Nowadays we are aware of women's history, social history and minority history and are much better equipped to create a shared history – one in which everyone can see the role of their own predecessors, and see beyond those predecessors only being of relevance if they became part of an elite. And there is no doubt that Scottish history itself has opened up over the last two decades under the guidance of teachers like Professors Edward J Cowan and Tom Devine, but I believe much still needs to be done.

Various friends have helped in the creation of this work, but I stress that none of them are to blame if you find any of the following offensive. It is more than likely some of you will, but I hope to stimulate debate rather than proscribe it. Thanks are due to Diana Brown, John Greig, Hugh McArthur, Ian McHardy, Davie Moir, Mandy Peat, Dougie Scott, Roderick McHardy and Nick Simpson all of whom have helped me figure things out. The crew at Luath were supportive, as is their wont, and as ever nothing would get done without the ongoing support of my wife Sandra Davidson. So thanks all but nae blame tae onie.

Notes

1 www.columbia.edu/itc/mealac/pritchett/oogenerallinks/ macaulay/txt_minute_education_1835.html
2 www.orkneyjar.com/archaeology/nessofbrodgar/

CHAPTER ONE

First Steps

ON 12 DECEMBER 1992, a march was held in Edinburgh, calling for the institution of a Scottish Parliament. The Democracy March, as it was known, set off from the point where Waterloo Place meets Regent Road. The Vigil for a Scottish Parliament had been in permanent occupation of a site just outside the Old Royal High School since 10 April that year. The demonstration was supported by many groups, such as Common Cause, the Trade Unions, the suspiciously short-lived Scotland United and a host of others. What was clear was that the demonstration had wide support and over 25,000 people turned up, a figure that the local constabulary, as ever, disputed. Obviously, such a momentous event attracted considerable media coverage and there were journalists and TV crews from many countries there that day.

One of the things that the media in general like is an anniversary, and 12 December 1992 was in fact a remarkable one. Precisely 200 years earlier, less than a half a mile away, a meeting had been arranged by the Societies of the Friends of the People. They had called a Convention to discuss their plans for increasing the demand for Democratic Reform. Scotland at the time was a one-man despotism run by Henry Dundas, who exercised absolute patronage over all levels of Scottish life on behalf of the Government in Westminster. The upshot of the Convention was that a group of men who became known as the Political Martyrs were transported to Botany Bay for sedition, defined as *Conduct or speech inciting people to rebel against the authority of a state or monarch*. It was felt by the hardy souls of the Vigil that the Scottish media should be made aware of this remarkable anniversary.

The Vigil Cairn, Calton Hill

Accordingly, every news outlet in the city received a document drawing their attention to this important historical fact. Mention came there none. Perhaps the document should have been delivered to the foreign news agencies. There is never any need to censor those who are eager to censor themselves.

Five years after the Democracy March, a very interesting conference was held at Moray House College of Education in Edinburgh. Moray House, now part of the University of Edinburgh, is situated just off the High Street, Edinburgh's Royal Mile and virtually in the shadow of Calton Hill on its south side. This conference titled *The Stert o a New Sang?* was called to discuss the need for teaching the Scots language and Scottish History in Scottish schools. Since 1872, both Scots and our other indigenous language, Gaelic, had been proscribed from education. The 1872 Education Act stipulated that the language of education in Scotland was to be English. Scots' existence as a separate language from English is historically unarguable and it, like Gaelic at the time, was the first language of many Scottish people, learned at their mother's knee. No matter, the education of the country was to be in English. Until the conference in 1997, this situation had remained essentially unchallenged. The other topic considered by the conference was the teaching of Scottish history. Those of us lucky enough to be taught Scottish history before this time owe a great deal of gratitude to our teachers, who chose to tell us something of our own past. It was not a part of the official curriculum, and in fact teaching Scottish history to Scottish children only became the norm after the institution of the Curriculum for Excellence in 2011, something which most of our European cousins find unbelievable. The conference eventually voted on a motion that the teaching of Scots language and Scottish history should be introduced into Scottish schools, and the motion received an approval rating of over 96 per cent. The conference was attended by teachers, advisers and a range of other educationalists, so it is safe to say they knew what they were doing. As an instance of that, the support for the teaching of Scots was not some politically driven proto-nationalist statement, but founded on the well-established educational practice of recognising the language a child brings to school. If you dismiss that language you effectively dismiss the child's social background and personal history, and in all too many instances blight their chances of developing to their full potential. Considerable research into this had previously been done amongst a range of minority language communities in various parts of Continental Europe. The conference had been organised under the aegis of the Scottish Consultative Council on the Curriculum and had been led by one of its Assistant Directors, the late, and much missed, Robbie Robertson. In time, Robbie submitted a report of the conference to the SCCC board. They rejected it, and demanded a rewrite. Robbie rewrote the report, which was rejected for a second time then shelved.

As a result of this, Robbie wrote an article called 'The Lang Clartie Rig' which was published in the magazine, *Education in the North*, in 1998. In it, he referred to the board of the SCCC as Gatekeepers, arguing that:

> While nothing can be said about individuals' ideological orientations, it is clear that Council, having been appointed by the previous administration's Secretary of State, is unlikely to be in any way radical or to attach any positive significance to Scottish culture.

The Democracy March and the Conference at Moray House took place five years apart, and I was actively involved in both. By the time of the Conference, I was the Director of the Scots Language Resource Centre and had been active participant in the Vigil for a Scottish Parliament since it started in 1992. I had also been involved for several years, through the Pictish Arts Society, in trying to increase interest in the Picts, so had a track record of sorts even then. The response of both the media to the march and the board of the SCCC to the conference brought to a head something that I had been aware of for a considerable time. Scottish history as it has been written over the past 300 years has all too often been subjected to suppression, distortion or manipulation by those who were in positions of importance, at both university and school level. Thankfully, since the inception of the Scottish Parliament and the election of a Nationalist government, the problem has begun to be addressed. But there is a long, long way to go. This book is an attempt to open up various areas of our past that have been manipulated by those gatekeepers with the clear intention of trying to make Scotland's past conform to essentially Britishist notions that see the south-east of England as the primary, perhaps only, focus of importance within the United Kingdom. That this section of Scottish society still has influence can be seen by the recent brouhaha over Alasdair Gray's use of the word 'coloniser' in the title of a recent essay. Never mind what he was actually saying in the essay, here was an uppity Jock spouting vile anti-Englishness according to this sad clique. Such ideas are common in certain sections of contemporary society. As American academic Richard Blaustein points out:

> [T]he Scottish lairds deliberately stripped themselves of Gaelic language [and Scots] and culture in their eagerness to assume metropolitan English values and norms, voluntarily committing ethnocide and linguicide.[1]

As Burns suggested, 'tae see oorsels as ithers see us' may indeed be a boon.

Blaustein's words seem to me to be a perfectly reasonable description and the hold that the landed classes have had over Scotland's governance over the period of Union has been a pernicious one. I would suggest that this espousal of metropolitan, or more properly, metrovincial (a prejudiced mindset typical of those considering themselves to be metropolitan elites, evinced by their ignorance of alternate modes of thinking), mores on the part of Scotland's ruling classes since then has essentially created a situation in which Scotland has been governed in what is virtually a colonial fashion. Until very recently, Scotland was directly ruled by a Secretary of State. The difference between the Secretary of State for Scotland and Governor-General of one of the Dominions of the British Empire never seemed to me to be great.

In his classical work of anti-colonialism, *The Wretched of the Earth* (1961), Frantz Fanon argues that:

> Perhaps we have not sufficiently demonstrated that colonialism is not simply content to impose its rule upon the present and the future of a dominated country. Colonialism is not merely satisfied with holding a people in its grip and emptying the native's brain of all form and content. By a kind of perverted logic, it turns to the past of the oppressed people and distorts, disfigures and destroys it. This work of devaluing pre-colonial history takes on a dialectal significance today.

> When we consider the efforts made to carry out the cultural estrangement so characteristic of the colonial epoch, we realise that nothing has been left to chance and that the total result looked for by colonial domination was indeed to convince the natives that colonialism came to lighten their darkness. The effect consciously sought by colonialism was to drive into the natives' heads the idea that if the settlers were to leave, they would at once fall back into barbarism, degradation and bestiality.[2]

The point here is that Scotland's past has been distorted and disfigured, if not destroyed, the clear hoped-for effect being that the historical differences between Scotland and England are diminished, while similarities are enhanced and even superimposed.

I believe that, at the dawn of a new millennium, it is time to shine a light on those areas of Scotland's history which have been customised, one way or another, to conform to the notion of Britishness, and try to see who we really are, warts and all. Only that way can we hope to have a story to tell coming generations of Scots children that is truly reflective of who *we* are.

It has to be said that history is a complicated process. As I have already said, the old cliché that the past is another country can be extended – it is another country for which we have no map. All history and prehistory is speculative to some extent. The historian, of course, relies primarily on written sources and there lies one of our major problems. It is true that due to invasions by Vikings and the English, and destructive rioting at the time of the Reformation, much of what had been written in Scotland in earlier times was destroyed. This has led to a reliance on external sources, which has given rise to certain ongoing problems that will be considered throughout this book. Two major problems are the slavish acceptance of Roman and Christian sources without subjecting them to proper criticism. This is not a value judgement, merely recognition that the mindset of people writing what we have come to think of as history is as important as what they actually say. The Romans were unashamedly propagandistic and the early Christian scribes, who left us what are often the only sources for particular times and events, were driven not by any notion of creating an objective historical record but of worshipping their God. That attitude was at the very core of founding our universities and though modern Scotland is a largely secular society, we have to recognise that this was not so in the past and that the effect of religion on people's perceptions of the past, and their present, must be factored into any understanding we wish to develop of the past.

A further problem we face is that the focus of most history to date is unapologetically elitist. In the years since the Second World

War, we have seen the development of social history, women's history and minority history, all of which were unheard of before that. However, history was, and for many still is, the study of the behaviour of elites – and here the new curriculum in England and Wales proposed by the recent British minister for Education, Michael Gove, is a clear example. And not just elites – most history before the 20th century only includes women when they are effectively doing a man's job. This concentration on the machinations of powerful men in politics, religion or the military has spread from history into pre-history. Indeed, archaeologists seem obsessed with analysing every new breakthrough as being the result of elitist behaviour. I will return to this point. Partially, of course, this bias arises because universities themselves are elitist institutions. In British terms, this means that there is a strong link between class and history – how many of our leading authorities over the years came from privileged backgrounds, bringing with them the prejudices and limitations of an education system designed to further the interests of their elite group? This is not an exaggeration. In the British media, concentrated in London, which in many ways has taken over the role that religion use to play in society, the vast majority of the highest level of jobs are held by people with public school and Oxbridge backgrounds. Their education rarely contains sufficient training in critical thinking to help offset the blinkered thinking that such an upbringing instils.

There are other ways of interpreting the past than constantly seeking to show that everything of value that ever happened was the result of elitist behaviour. And in Scottish terms, this is of some importance, as we shall see. My bias is towards understanding the past in terms of communal behaviour and it may be that I have a tendency to exaggerate the role of communal behaviour – well, the pendulum has swung one way too long and I hope in this series of essays that I can do something to redress that.

Stewart Kermack's idea of a forensic approach to historical

documentation strikes me as eminently sensible, for it leads to one testing not just what was written, but who wrote it, and why. There is an old historical chestnut that problems can be solved by asking, *cui buono*? Who profits? I think that this, combined with something of a forensic approach is the way to go forward in trying to elucidate a clearer picture of Scotland's past. I go even further. Historians abhor 'story', by which I mean local traditions that refer to mythical, legendary, potentially historical and historical events, people, even place-names. The old cliché that history is written by the winners, while true, ignores the reality that unless the losers are wiped out, they will continue to speak to each other about personal and communal experiences – they will tell stories. This, of course, was much more prevalent before literacy became common, which even in Scottish terms only started to happen in the 17th century. Stories can preserve reality over millennia and local traditions can preserve data that has been ignored elsewhere. The well-known instance of Heinrich Schliemann finding Troy by following Homer's 'stories' against the advice of historians and pre-historians has still not been truly appreciated over a century and a half later. Partly, of course, this is as a result of the same elite attitudes already referred to – how could the common folk know more than their betters? Well, as I believe I have no betters – and that I am better than no one else – I find such an idea risible. Story, because it arises out of communal activity, has a resonance that the written word cannot aspire to. At one level, story can be understood as a distilling of communal experience, and the idea that all story is no more than Chinese whispers is nonsensical. Stories within traditional communities may vary from teller to teller, but the core of their sense always remains. This is something essentially human and we see it in children, individually, and in groups, asking time and again for the same story. This leads to a familiarity with stories that means they cannot be altered at whim. They survive because they attain a form which is fit for purpose, and though variations will always occur (repetition by rote is only a small part of traditional story-telling), the core remains. It has psycho-sociological relevance. This is not to say that traditional tales are always historically accurate – that is not their purpose – but they can shed light on the past. A word of caution, though: just as history has to be subjected to critical thinking, so must story.

My interpretation of some of the periods that will be considered in this book, such as the post-Culloden period, derive directly from following up traditional stories which suggested that standard history wasn't telling anything like the full story. Likewise, my interpretation of the far past, and the proposed existence of a distinct Scottish mythology rooted in primal religion, comes from material generally considered outside the remit of the historian and archaeologist. Time and again, I will return to the role of story in preserving what people believed was important because stories only survive if they continue to be told, and they only continue to be told if they have relevance to both the teller and the audience. J. Edward Chamberlin, Professor of English and Comparative Literature at the University of Toronto, opened his recent book, *If This is Your Land, Where Are Your Stories?* (2004), with the story of a meeting between natives of British Columbia and some government officials intent on appropriating the land they lived on.[3] One of the elders asked a simple question, 'If this is your land, where are your stories?' The officials did not know what he meant. They were concerned with giving deeds for the lands in question to incoming white men and thus stealing them from people who had lived on, and lived with, this land for untold generations. And their history, their sense of self, was in their stories. In the words of Woody Guthrie, 'Some will rob you with a six-gun/And some with a fountain pen'.[4] Nowadays, we are educated in schools and think of knowledge as dependent on literacy. It is not, and just because something is written down does not mean it is true. In historical terms, the Second World War was won by whom? The American and Russian versions differ, never mind what the Germans and Japanese think.

Traditional culture has survived in Scotland, despite Anglicisation, Americanisation (Hollywoodisation?) and the growth of seemingly endlessly inventive modern media. And we retain our stories. In this respect, the paucity of early Scottish written sources means also that in terms of mythology and legend, too much has been made over the past 200 years of the influence of other cultures on Scotland, particularly Ireland. As I hope I will show, the influence of Irish culture on Scottish history is not only vastly over-rated, its role was exaggerated as a specific propaganda project that has a deleterious effect on our understanding of Scotland's past as a whole. That is not to gainsay that the cultural interpenetration of those parts of the world we think of as Scotland and Ireland go back millennia. Having two Irish great-grandparents myself, I am well aware of our connections, but as Ewan Campbell pointed out in 2000, there is no evidence to actually support the notion that the Scots come from Ireland.[5] *Cui buono*? We shall see.

This is not a history book; it is an attempt to adopt a new way of approaching the history of this small nation, a history that has been subsumed by the interests of the larger nation, with whom we became entangled three centuries ago. For centuries before that, Scotland looked to the south in fear. Whether it was Romans, Northumbrians or English, it was from the south that the armies came. We had also had to learn to deal with the Vikings, but that seems to have resulted in an accommodation that gave rise to a specifically rich cultural period, that of the Gall-Gael and the later development of the Lordship of the Isles. The idea that the Scots were as indigenous as the Picts may also lead to a potential for seeing the roots of the Lordship of the Isles as being much older even than the 'Kingdom' of Dalriada. This brings me to probably the most ridiculous rewriting of Scotland's history – the so-called Wars of Independence. I believe that this term is an insult to every native-born Scot and is a clear example of what Fanon said about colonial history. The clear subtext of this phrase is obviously to suggest that Scotland had to win its independence from England. The reality is that Scotland was a nation state before England and, despite the Machiavellian behaviour of various English kings, Scotland was never part of England. The opposite cannot be said to be true as, at various times, the Border was considerably south of where it currently sits. Yet, generations of Scottish historians have been happy to peddle this egregious subtext. This is as clear an example of the gatekeeper mentality as you could wish to have. And it is not just in the distant past that such distortions have taken place. The current incumbent of Buckingham Palace is referred to as Elizabeth II of Great Britain – there never has been an Elizabeth I of Great Britain. Similarly, the Duke of Windsor was called Edward VIII of Great Britain on his coronation in 1936, when the only previous Edwards were kings of England. So what? The English love their Warrior Queen and wanted to hark back to her glorious reign when Lizzie Windsor came to the throne and what did the realities of Scottish, or even English, history matter? And the gatekeepers gratefully tugged their forelocks in agreement. A small thing, perhaps, but when we have a government in Westminster actively trying to resurrect an essentially British imperialist curriculum for schools in England and Wales, such things are straws in the wind.

As should be obvious by now, I am not a believer in objective history – the very idea is intellectually nonsensical. None of us can be different than we are and our ideas of who we are and where we come from will always influence how we see and interpret the past. I do try to consider all relevant facts but cannot remove myself from my writing and have no wish to do so. What motivates me is an attempt to understand the past of the country

I was born in and, after a lifetime of reading, debating and lecturing on the subject, I have come to the conclusion that not only is there much distortion in Scottish history, but also that the models that have been used to try and elucidate that past are not helpful. If we want to ensure that future generations of Scottish bairns have access to as good a picture of the past as we can manage to give them, it is time we looked to that past itself to help us analyse it better and not what happened elsewhere, in Rome, Athens, Cairo or London. As the technical capacities of the natives of Orkney in the far past (shown by the excavations at Ness of Brodgar) make abundantly clear, this part of the world was not, is not, and will not be, a peripheral backwater in the story of the human race in Europe and the world.

Notes

1   Blaustein R; *The Thistle and the Brier: Historical Links and Cultural Parallels Between Scotland and Appalachia*; McFarland & Company; Jefferson, North Carolina; 2003. p. 59.

2   Fanon, F; *The Wretched of the Earth*; Presence Africaine; Paris; 1963. p. 170.

3   Chamberlin, JE; *If This is Your Land, Where Are Your Stories*; Carcanet; Manchester; 2006.

4   Guthrie, W; 'Pretty Boy Floyd'; Smithsonian Folkways; 1944.

5   Campbell. E; 'Were the Scots Irish?' in *Antiquity*, vol. 75, number 288; 2000. pp. 285–292.

CHAPTER TWO

The Far Past

RECENTLY THERE HAS been much excitement about the excavations at the Ness of Brodgar on the mainland of Orkney, where a truly monumental series of discoveries have been made.[1] Within the immediate area, there are of course other significant prehistoric monuments, which include the magnificent Stone circles of Stenness and Brodgar, and the great tomb of Maes Howe. Evidence has been uncovered of monumental stone buildings within what is clearly a ritual enclosure dating from around 3000BCE, half a millennium before Stonehenge and Avebury were raised in the south of England, or the first of the great pyramids

Carlin Maggie

built in Egypt. Earlier structures on the Brodgar site have been dated as being in use from 3600BCE. It has long been a cornerstone of Received Opinion that 'civilisation' started in Egypt and Greece and only slowly spread outwards, eventually reaching the benighted natives of these islands. This Mediterranean-centric thinking has been dominant for far too long. The fact that Brodgar was closely matched by roughly contemporaneous megalithic – big stone – sites at Calanais on Lewis and Kilmartin in Argyll (not forgetting Ireland's Boyne tombs) tells a completely different story. Yet, although the concept of the megalithic culture, having started in Orkney, was first mooted by Professor Stuart Piggott in the 1950s, it has never been taken seriously till now. Even such a recent and interesting book as *Facing the Ocean* (2001) by Professor Barry Cunliffe, which looks at prehistoric sea travel and trade in Western Europe, paid virtually no attention to any locations in Scotland. Yet, the evidence clearly suggests the people in and around Brodgar were in contact with other societies in the British Isles and potentially far beyond. The closing down of a major temple at Brodgar is believed to have involved the feeding of thousands of people at one time.[2] This suggests that many people had come a long way to take part in this communal event, as the entire population of the Orkneys at the time is unlikely to have been anything close to this amount. You only see what you are looking for, and the truth of the matter is that the notion of civilisation coming north has long been entrenched in the educational institutions of Western Europe. At a lecture on the Ness of Brodgar in March 2013, the archaeologist in charge, the inspirational Nick Card, made what I believe is a telling point. He observed that a group of contemporaneous structures uncovered at Brodgar were all different, but within the same generic type. He suggested that they may have been seasonally used ritual centres for a series of different kin-groups. This corresponds to suggestions throughout this book that we should be interpreting much of Scotland's past as essentially tribal. By this, I mean that considerable areas of the country were still occupied by people whose socio-economic structure was that of a kin-based society, which saw itself as inherently self-sustaining. Tribalism is often presented as being exclusive i.e. keeping people out, but from the point of view of their members, they are specifically inclusive. In later times, this was called clan society. The lack of urban developments

Calanais Stones

before David 1's institution of the burghs was echoed subsequently throughout most of Scotland until just a couple of hundred years ago by the survival of early fermtouns in the Lowlands, and *bailes* in the Highlands, meaning that most of the population still lived in small, inter-related communities that had strong kinship links.

At all of these sites, there is undeniable evidence of solar and lunar alignments and the main stone circle at Calanais is aligned to observe the 18.6-year occurrence of what is known as the lunar standstill, with another such site in Kilmartin Glen.[3] This is the point where the moon's path is at its farthest south and then two weeks later at its farthest north.

Although more work remains to be done on the solar and lunar alignments on Orkney, there can be little doubt that all three sites were developed by people who were aware of some level of mathematics and astronomy. The late Professor Alexander Thom's interpretation of such sites as showing advanced mathematics has not stood the sense of time. Basic solar and lunar alignments require some level of observation but not trigonometry. The old and increasingly discredited archaeological interpretation of this is, of course, that there was some astronomer-priestly elite who were bossing everyone else around to create these places. I would suggest that his is yet another unfortunate hangover from the masculine, hierarchical, militaristic bias of academic thinking that has proven so wrong up till now. Throughout the world, people gather together for ritual activity, often on hill-top sites, and those whose role it is to conduct such ceremonies do not have to have a stratified role in society. Status does not always have to mean either power over others, or wealth.

The evidence found in Scotland can be interpreted to tell a different story. Within the structure of communal, kin-based societies, also known as tribes and clans, there are a whole range of processes whereby people can have status without it making them anyone else's superior. Even chiefs are part of the kin-groups that form tribes, not above or apart from them. The process by which Scottish crofters still come together when there is need for large-scale communal activities without any 'leadership' is a living reflection of this enduring way of life.

If the idea that the megalithic culture actually spread out from Orkney (or possibly one of the other northern locations), is true, it suggests that sea travel was an everyday fact of life in Scotland 5,000 years ago. We have no hard evidence of boats from that far back, but it is quite possible that the vessels of the time were made of skin. After all, Inuit peoples were hunting whales in skin boats till relatively recently and such vessels have been known to travel thousands of miles. The earliest European wooden boat, from Ferriby in Yorkshire, is dated to almost 2000BCE.[4] Some commentators have drawn attention to the fact that the style of that boat is akin to early vessels from Egypt. Previously, this would have been seen as clear evidence that the Egyptians came to Britain. What the evidence could equally support is that the sea-traveling, megalithic-raising people of the British Isles might have travelled in the opposite direction. For those educated to think of the Classical and Christian worlds as being the fount of all knowledge, it is perhaps difficult to come to terms with all this, but the evidence is clear. We can postulate travel from Orkney, or the Hebrides, to Greece and even Africa 5,000 years ago. And there is no need to go further and claim that influence from this part of the world became dominant elsewhere. Cultures interact, just as individuals and kin groups do.

What the evidence does strongly suggest is that a sophisticated megalithic-building society formed in Scotland before 3000BCE. The timescale of this society's development is still a mystery, but it did not happen overnight and may well have its roots millennia earlier. After all, people had come north millennia earlier than that after the retreat of the ice, the earliest human artefacts found in Scotland having been dated to circa 12000BCE.[5]

This completely changes the Mediterranean-centric picture of prehistory that has effectively been Received Opinion in Europe for over a millennium and a half, although it is patently clear that when the ice retreated at the end of the last Ice Age that people did come north. It was well over 10,000 years ago, and in that time it is clear that society developed in interesting and important ways here in the north, as well as around the Mediterranean.

It also means that certain ancient records must be re-evaluated in light of this new evidence. There are early Greek records mentioning one Abaris, a Hyperborean who is said to have met with Pythagoras[6] and later Classical writers mention a circular temple in Hyperborea.[7] Several authors, interpreting Hyperborea as referring to the British Isles, have suggested that the references must be to Stonehenge, but as we know that that particular monument was raised after, and influenced by, the work of the megalith builders of Brodgar, we must challenge that particular assumption. The Greek writer Herodotus mentions Abaris in the middle of the 1st millennium BCE, and Herodotus was born ten years after Pythagoras died. Does this mean that the Hyperborean temple still had an active priesthood circa 500BCE? If so, was it Calanais or Brodgar, or elsewhere? It may also be that what Herodotus was doing was recounting a story of something that had happened earlier, perhaps a visit from a Hyperborean priest. We know that story itself can carry actual verifiable data over tens of thousands of years without the need of writing, so it is not impossible.[8] However, the fact that Herodotus was born only ten years after Pythagoras is believed to have died reinforces the idea that he is reporting a relatively recent event. And did Pythagoras develop his mathematical understanding with help from the north? If so, can we see this as evidence of an ongoing use of such sites?

In the past, much was written about the supposed influence of cultures such as that in Malta having influenced the megalith builders of Western Europe – perhaps we have to turn this around in the light of new understanding.

However it is not just Pythagoras who has been said to have had contact with this part of the world. Over the past couple of decades, a theory has been developed that Odysseus, after the fall of Troy, circa 1200BCE, travelled not through the Aegean islands but through the Hebrides. This would, of course, account for the fact that it was seven years before he returned home to his wife, Penelope. Ed Furlong suggested that the original whirlpool of Scylla and Charybdis in Homer's *Odyssey*, was inspired by the Corryvreckan between Scarba and Jura.[9]

The Corryvreckan is located directly opposite Kilmartin and has its own legendary existence.[10] As we shall see below, some of these legends may reflect beliefs that were part of the culture of the people who raised the megaliths, here and elsewhere. It may also be relevant that the Roman poet Plutarch, writing in the 1st century CE, tells us that the father of the Greek Pantheon of Gods, Zeus, imprisoned his own father Kronos in a cave on an island, which some have interpreted as being in the Hebrides.[11] In light of our expanding knowledge of megalithic culture in Scotland, all these references must surely be reconsidered. The Greeks and Romans, of course, had the written word long before the people here did, but if there was contact – which is a two-way process – is it feasible that some of this material in Classical literature originated here? The idea that because people are not literate they are not intelligent or knowledgeable is plainly bizarre.

The fact that we have a series of significant ritual sites dating from around and before 3000BCE means that society here at that time was culturally sophisticated. The idea that we only ever inherited cultural developments from other places is no longer tenable. The much-vaunted creativity of Scots from the Enlightenment onwards appears to have deep roots indeed. This has other ramifications. I have suggested elsewhere that the society we think of as Pictish was directly descended from these earlier peoples, as there is no hard evidence that there ever was a major invasion of people into Scotland between 3000BCE and Roman times.[12] This probably means that communication with other parts of mainland Europe and beyond was continuous throughout the period, and there is archaeological evidence to sustain this. However, there is also the fact that in the megalithic period a great deal of rock art was created. This was not just cup-and-ring marks but involved a variety of designs, including carvings of deer in Kilmartin and at Ballochmyle in Ayrshire. Deer also figure extensively on the later Pictish Symbol Stones, and we should perhaps consider the possibility that there is a continuity of meaning from one to the other.[13] The dating of rock carving is difficult, and most dating of Pictish stones has been on the grounds that they are artefacts of what may be described as the Pictish state, coming into existence in the centuries after the Romans departed the southern half of Britain. They have been dated mainly on the grounds of comparison with carvings outside Scotland. Given the realisation that Scotland was so culturally developed in the far past, should we not be considering whether the Class I, pre-Christian, stones of the Picts may have a much earlier gestation than has been accepted to date? We were not at the periphery of human society in the far past, so it is about time we stopped trying to understand ourselves through comparison with what happened elsewhere and started developing an understanding of our past from indigenous evidence. The classification of the Pictish Symbol Stones was part of the monumental work, *Early Christian Monuments of Scotland*, originally published in 1903 (and in a paperback version 100 years later by Pinkfoot Press). It clearly included a considerable number of stones that were pre-Christian and it may be time that we started seeing those particular works as part of the continuum that preceded Christianity, and potentially originated in megalithic times. I have suggested elsewhere that the term Picts was used, by the Romans at least, to mean all the tribal peoples north of Hadrian's Wall, and thus there are grounds for recategorising carved stones from outside of the generally accepted Pictish areas, such as those at Govan, Eggerness and Trusty's Hill, as basically Pictish. I would go further and suggest that we look beyond Pictish designation and consider the entire continuum of rock art from megalithic to the arrival of Christianity, as a whole, to see what continuities can be discerned.

Caesar said that the Gaulish druids went north to Britain for their training and, given the highly sophisticated ritual sites in the north and west of Scotland, did they come all the way north? We know that certain prehistoric sites were used and reused over considerable periods of time. The idea of cultural continuity to much later periods must also be tested. Should we think of the Picts, the Britons and the Scots as the direct cultural descendants of the megalithic builders? Recent DNA testing shows that many contemporary Scots are directly linked to such early peoples. Such ideas need to be tested, just as many more sites in Scotland have to be archaeologically investigated so we can know more of who we are.

It is a fact that until the end of the 20th century, at least half of the archaeology done in Scotland was at Roman sites. How much more do we need to know about the campaigns and short-scale occupations of the Romans? Our native archaeology cries out for more exploration, whether it be in deep prehistory, the 1st millennium CE or later. We still know little about whole periods of our past and devoting scarce resources to temporary invaders is just another reflection of an outdated and essentially colonialist attitude towards that past. The Romans brought us literacy, but with it a great deal of baggage that, frankly, we no longer need.

Notes

1   www.orkneyjar.com/archaeology/nessofbrodgar/
2   www.orkneyjar.com/archaeology/nessofbrodgar/excavation-background-2/a-millennium-of-activity/
3   Scott, D; *Watchers of the Dawn*; CD; 2001. p. 248. For more information, contact douglas.scottt@btinternet.com
4   www.ferribyboats.co.uk/dating/index.html
5   www.redorbit.com/news/science/1669072/flints_from_12000_bc_found_in_scotland/
6   en.wikipedia.org/wiki/Abaris_the_Hyperborean
7   en.wikipedia.org/wiki/Hyperborea
8   Isaacs, J; *Australian Dreaming: 40,000 Years of Aboriginal History*; Landsdowne Publishing Pty; Naremburn 1980. p. 15.
9   Furlong, E; *Where Did Odysseus Go?*; CreateSpace; USA; 2012.
10 www.whirlpool-scotland.co.uk/cailleach.html
11 penelope.uchicago.edu/Thayer/E/Roman/Texts/Plutarch/Moralia/De_defectu_oraculorum*.html
12 McHardy, SA; *A New History of the Picts*; Luath; Edinburgh; 2011.
13 McHardy, SA; *The Pagan Symbols of the Picts*; Luath; Edinburgh; 2012. p. 82.

CHAPTER THREE

An Indigenous Mythology?

WHILE THERE ARE shared ideas with our Irish and Scandinavian neighbours, there is evidence that suggests that the indigenous mythology of tribal Scotland's primal religion was rooted in our own landscape in a unique fashion.

History is not the only window on the past. Most cultures have inherited a mythology from earlier times. Lewis Spence defines myth as:

> an account of the deeds of a god or supernatural being usually expressed in terms of primitive thought; It is an attempt to explain the relations of man to the universe, and it has for those who recount it a predominantly religious value; or it may have arisen to explain the existence of some social organization, a custom, or the peculiarities of an environment.[1]

Leaving aside the reference to 'primitive thought' on the basis that our ancestors were no less intellectually able than we are, this serves as reasonable explanation for what we think of as mythology. Particularly in the pre-literate world, myths were used to describe the physical world – in terms of human behaviour – so they could be easily understood, not least by children and young people. Mythological stories were usually told within the specific environment of the audience, which accounts for widespread and varied instances of accounts of mythical figures, like 'King' Arthur, stories of whom were told wherever the P-Celtic languages were spoken in Britain, and Brittany, or Finn MacCoul, whose stories belong to the Q-Celtic Irish, Manx and Scots. P-Celtic is the designation given to Welsh and Breton, their predecessors, and to the recently revived Cornish, while Q-Celtic is used to describe Irish, Scottish Gaelic, their predecessors, and the recently revived Manx. The Britons of Strathclyde, the Gododdin of Lothian and most, if not all, of the Picts are believed to have spoken early forms of P-Celtic. In terms of Britain, the general approach has been to see the both Germanic and Celtic groups of myth as originating in England and Ireland. Germanic myths are understood as being related to what we nowadays think of as Norse mythology. Nineteenth-century nationalism has left a residue of identifying such material not only with language but with ethnicity, the intellectual convolutions of white supremacist groups showing how dangerous this can be. Of course, the very idea of ethnicity is problematic. The categories of ethnicity that arose in the period of Western imperialist expansion are, to put it mildly, ill-defined if not downright daft. To lump together the Ibo of Nigeria, the Masai of Kenya and the San of southern Africa as Negroid, for example, illustrates the point. Likewise, using the term Asiatic to describe the Ainu of Japan, the Khmer of Cambodia and the Banjara of India is pointless, unless of course the point is to simply mark these people out as non-Caucasian. In Scottish terms, the common sense approach to all of this is to simply say 'We are aw Jock Tamson's bairns', though I prefer to think of us as Jock Tamson's mongrel bastards. The idea of any kind of racial purity, while perhaps having some relevance amongst dog and cattle breeders, does not help human inter-relationships.

All peoples have their own mythology, of course, but the mythologies that are generally reckoned to be relevant to Scotland – Norse, Celtic, Germanic – have a problem that has recently only begun to be appreciated. I have pointed out the potentially limiting effects of Christian Classical education on interpreting history. The same can be said of mythology, for the influence of the pantheon of Greek mythology on those who first wrote down what we think of as the different mythologies of north-western

Europe has been considerable. In Scottish terms, the problem is confounded by the fact that we clearly have traditions, not only of King Arthur, which we share with other P-Celtic speaking peoples, and Finn MacCoul, which we share with the Q-Celtic speakers, but also considerable traces of what appear to be Norse-inspired mythological thinking. However, in one of the beings we share with the Irish, and in other forms with the Norse, we can perhaps see the beginnings of something else.

One of the reasons I started looking for traces an indigenous mythology was the fact that there are hardly any references to Scotland at all in what were the standard texts for 'Celtic Studies' when I was younger – *Pagan Celtic Britain*,[2] *Celtic Heritage*[3] and *The Celtic Realms*.[4] This seemed totally bizarre. There is no argument about the fact that a Celtic-speaking, warrior, tribal society lived on in Scotland until the 18th century. However, while the authors of these works were happy to talk about the tribal activities reported in early Irish sagas or stories of the apparently legendary Arthur among the P-Celtic speakers and Finn among the Q-Celtic speakers, there was no mention of the cultural relevance of the Highland clans. This is bizarre, but it can be seen as part of an ongoing deliberate blindness to the actual cultural existence of Scotland as a separate historical entity. Received Opinion is a powerful beastie!

The idea that the megalithic culture could have started here is perhaps also relevant to mythological thinking. At Calanais, the main circle aligns on the 18.6-year lunar standstill. The physical location of the standstill point is in a range of hills to the south of Loch Roag. That range of hills has the shape of a recumbent female figure and is known as the *Cailich na Mointeach* – the old woman of the moors. The great ritual landscape of Kilmartin overlooks the site of the world's third-biggest whirlpool and this is linked in legend with another old woman of the same name, the Cailleach. I have been assured on several occasions by linguists

Cailich na Mointeach

that there is absolutely no link between the first syllable of Calanais and those of the Cailich/Cailleach. The relative sounds made by the letter 'l' in each name are totally different, they tell me, in modern Gaelic. As to what they were 5,000 years ago, how can they tell? There is also the fact that Scotland too has Cailiness, a promontory on the south-eastern coast of the Rhinns of Galloway. There is no reclining Cailleach here, but there is a cluster of prehistoric monuments, including a stone circle, enclosures, cairns and a mound, and flint axe-heads and burial cists have been found here. It seems to have been another area of ritual activity for some form of primal religion. One of the place-names nearby is Kirkmaiden which, as we shall see, is also significant.

The Cailleachs at Calanais and near Kilmartin are far from the only ones in Scotland. There are many Gaelic tales of the Cailleach Bheur – the Biting Hag – who is often interpreted as the personification of winter, and for a long time the laziness of Received Opinion has seen this creature as having derived from the Irish Cailleach Bheur. However, it has long been known that there are many more Cailleach place-names and stories of her in Scotland than in Ireland and, as we shall see, the influence of Irish Gaelic culture on Scotland has been vastly overstated for far too long. Many of the Cailleachs in Scotland are particularly associated with mountains.[5] These are often significant mountains like Ben Nevis, Lochnagar, Ben Wyvis and Ben Cruachan, and she actually has several mountains named after her. She is also known as a weather-worker and as the actual creator of much of the landscape. Her name originally meant 'the veiled one', and that is a good description of many of the mountains she is linked with. She is, in short, a goddess figure and in one story at least, has the power of restoring life.[6] In some other stories, she actually changes from being the Hag of Winter into Bride, the Goddess of Summer. This happens at Beltane, the traditional Gaelic May Day festival. One of the intriguing things about the Cailleach and Bride is that they are matched exactly by the Carlin and the Maiden in Scots tradition, and both languages preserve locations where the pairs are linked in the landscape.[7] I have mentioned that there are links to the Cailleach at Calanais and Kilmartin, but in Orkney, close to the Stones of Stenness, themselves just south of the Ness of Brodgar, is the magnificent chambered tomb of Maes Howe. Maes here is a variant of May's Howe, or mound, and May is Scots for Maiden. What we appear to have at these major sites and on breast-shaped hills (paps) and elsewhere throughout Scotland is a hint of a system of belief based on a dual-goddess figure. This worldview possibly underlay the rituals of the primal religion that took place at such sites. The single find (so far?) of the Westray Wifie is perhaps relevant to this.

In some instances in the landscape, the Cailleach seems to be linked not to Bride or the Maiden but to the Bodach, the Old Man

Westray Wifie

to her Old Woman. The root of Bodach is *bod*, a penis, which underlines that we are dealing with ancient notions of fertility. The two are linked at one of the country's most famous pre-Christian ritual sites – The Tigh na Bodach or Tigh na Cailleach at the foot of Glen Cailliche which runs into Glen Lyon in Perthshire.[8] No one knows for how long it has been going on, but every Beltane, three curiously shaped stones, perhaps representing the Cailleach, the Bodach and Bride, the daughter, are brought out from their little house and the house is re-thatched.

What all of this suggests is that there may well have been a distinct Scottish mythology based around the perception of a dual goddess figure, representing the basic life force of all things, a mythology that is rooted in the landscape and is truly indigenous. It may also be very old indeed, for recent research at Gobekli Tepe in modern Turkey has shown that the use of ritual sites actually pre-dated the development of fixed field agriculture.[9] Nomadic or semi-nomadic peoples interacted with various locations in the landscape over significant periods of time, and if this involved cutting back or burning certain vegetation to encourage growth for when they returned, we can think of those designated as hunter-gatherers as actually being farmers, if not settled ones. The development of fixed farming is of course said to have started in the Near East – like everything else – but as we have evidence of human occupation in Scotland from at least 12000BCE, perhaps there are other cornerstones of Received Opinion awaiting to be toppled.[10]

Given the length of occupation at so many of our early sites, we should also remember that the idea of 'ancestor worship', perhaps more properly understood as respect for those who preceded you, was to some extent based on the awareness that the knowledge that you did possess had been passed down to you from previous generations. After all, once you know where midsummer sun rises, you do not need a further generation of specialists to remind you, particularly if the alignment is already in place. And that knowledge was based on direct experience of the shared environment. The idea that it had to include a specialist class of dedicated sky-watchers is not the only interpretation. While it seems likely that there would have been some sort of religious operatives, these may have been more like shamanic participants rather than any structured and elite priesthood. The idea the human beings have to be led to do anything of communal value is simply rubbish.

In terms of the possibilities of there being an indigenous mythology in Scotland, that is, other than imports from other lands with which we have shared a great deal culturally over the millennia – one of the things to consider is what we could call non-standard religious or ritual practice. It may be impossible to date the commencement of such spectacular activities as the Burning of the Clavie at Burghead and the Stonehaven Fireball Ceremony, but they clearly have some relation to the widely reported Beltane (Mayday) and Samhain (Halloween) rites of earlier centuries. Even a ceremony like the pilgrimage to see the Midsummer sun on Lochnagar may have had its origins in the far past, but there are also other practices that suggest that in relatively recent historical times Scotland was not as homogenously Christian as is portrayed. One such instance was the bull sacrifice at Loch Maree in 1678.[11] It is perhaps better to think of these as survivals of primal religion rather than categorise them as 'pagan'. The term 'pagan' has too many connotations of modern practices and, though the re-institution of the Beltain and Samhain fires on Edinburgh's Calton Hill are extremely interesting, they do not have any link to the far past and are modern revivals, something which shows in much of the iconography associated with such events.

The bull sacrifice at Dingwall is echoed in reports from other parts of the country and suggests that the hold of ancient ways is tenacious. There are numerous references in Presbytery Records from the 16th and 17th centuries that show people attending wells, caves and other ancient sacred sites – the repetition of censure against so many individuals suggests that such activity was in fact relatively common after the first condemnations in the immediate post-Reformation period. Another example is the on-going attendances at the Clootie Well on the Black Isle.[12] Over the past few years, other wells and ancient sites have begun to attract the same kind of attention in different parts of Scotland, again a process of revival. However, underlying all the reports of well and cave visitations from the 16th and 17th centuries is something that may well have been of major importance – the much-reported activities of witches. Several modern analyses have seen the witches as always having been poor defenceless women persecuted out of fanatical religious zeal for their healing and herbal skills. While this is undoubtedly true in some, perhaps even most cases, there is some material that suggests a possible continuity with the primal religion. The independent scholar Eddie Murray has pointed out that the famous Auldearn witch, Isobel Gowdie, gave information on the workings of her coven willingly, and that some of the activities seem likely to have been remnants of ancient ritual.[13]

This can partly be explained in terms of human behaviour – if something was believed to have worked for your forefathers, it could work for you too, even if there were other newer method-ologies – why throw the baby out with the bath water? The wide-spread occurrence of the Guidman's Crofts – areas of land left uncultivated in honour of the Good Man, a.k.a. Auld Horny, an indigenous version of the Devil – shows how tenacious such prac-tices were.[14] Overall, they offered a kind of belt-and-braces approach where, although you can pray to the Christian God in Kirk on Sunday, there is nothing wrong with asking the help of somebody else too. All of this was still happening more than a thousand years after Scotland was, according to our historians,

Paps of Fife

Paps of Jura

completely Christianised and thus civilised. Behind the figure of the Guidman, Auld Horny, etc., there is perhaps something else. Can we trace out links between such 'pagan' behaviour and the primal religion I have suggested may well have been focused round the Mother Goddess?

Notes

1   Spence, L; *An Introduction to Mythology*; George G Harrop & Co; London; 1923. p. 11–12.

2   Ross, A; *Pagan Celtic Britain*; Academy Chicago Publishers; Chicago; 1996.

3   Rees, A and Rees, B; *Celtic Heritage*; Thames & Hudson; London; 1961.

4   Dillon, M and Chadwick, N; *The Celtic Realms*; Weidenfeld & Nicolson; London; 1967.

5   McHardy, SA; *On the Trail of Scotland's Myths and Legends*; Luath; Edinburgh 2005; p. 21f.

6   Campbell, JF; *Popular Tales of the West Highlands: Volume 2*; Birlinn; Edinburgh; 1994 (reprint); p. 85.

7   McNeill, M; *The Silver Bough*; Wm McLellan; Glasgow; 1959. p. 21.

8   canmore.rcahms.gov.uk/en/site/23898/details/tigh+nam+bodach/

9   en.wikipedia.org/wiki/Gobekli_Tepe

10 news.stv.tv/scotland/87708-scotlands-oldest-ever-human-settlement-discovered-in-biggar/

11 www.philipcoppens.com/lochmaree.html

12 www.undiscoveredscotland.co.uk/munlochy/clootiewell/index.html

13 stuartmchardy.wordpress.com/2013/04/02/isobel-gowdie/

14 witherlins.webs.com/customaryaccusations.htm
15 McHardy, SA; *The Pagan Symbols of the Picts*; Luath;
    Edinburgh; 2012. p. 135f.

CHAPTER FOUR

Between the Walls

OVER MANY YEARS, the idea has been put forward that the lands between Hadrian's Wall and the Antonine Wall were, to all intents and purposes, part of the Roman Empire. Or, if not actually within the Empire, they formed some sort of buffer state that was under the influence of Rome. Well, let's see.

The first attempt the Romans made at establishing a border in North Britain was in the time of Agricola, the supposed victor of the Battle of Mons Graupius. I say supposed, as it is bad historical practice to accept the veracity of a single source, and when it is a Roman source taken from a posthumous panegyric written by the subject's son-in-law, we are entitled to take a critical approach. According to our author, Tacitus, Agricola had come north to conquer the northern half of the island of Britain and the Caledonian tribes faced him in pitched battle. Although they outnumbered his troops by over three to one, Roman military tactics won the day and the natives fled into the woods and hills. I always found it a bit rich that they 'fled' back to where they actually lived. Tacitus needed to give his father-in-law a great victory. He also had to give Agricola a fitting opponent and, in the personage of Calgacus, the battle leader of the Caledonians, we see a very interesting creation, assuming that was what he was. He is no king and no noble and his name appears to mean either the Swordsman or the Bristly One, and it is perhaps not stretching a point to assume he was chosen to be the leader on the day because of his military skills. More than that, there is the fact that he said to talk of 'Freedom'.[1] Such language clearly comes from the tradition of Roman rhetoric, but it also lays down something with definite echoes in later Scottish history. The idea that people would fight for their freedom is, of course, perfectly normal, but in the figure of Calgacus, despite his attraction to so many future generations of Scots, it is difficult to avoid the idea that he is really no more than the Roman version of the Noble Savage.

Until the actual site of Mons Graupius is found and exca-vated, we cannot take Tacitus at his word, no matter how much Romanophiles like to. Also, you may wish to take a pinch of salt with the reported casualty figures: 10,000 Caledonians and 360 Romans. While it is conceivable that the Roman army, a highly trained and organised killing machine, would have caused mayhem against tribal warriors raised to fight one-on-one with what were effectively duelling weapons rather than the efficient killing technology of their enemies, the idea that they hung around long enough for 10,000 of their number to be killed is, as they say, pushing it a bit. It is also reminiscent of more modern times, echoing, for instance, the figures of enemy casualties that were pumped out by the American Government during the Vietnam War. The numbers of enemy dead would imply that there was virtually no population left.

Archaeological investigations have shown that in this period the Romans set up a series of forts along the Gask ridge, which runs south-east to north-west along the northern side of Srath-earn towards Perth.[2] The forts appear to have been built as part of a major project and were placed opposite the glens running north into the mountains. They did not last long and were aban-doned by 85CE. Given that they were linked by a series of signal stations, it is likely that this was the first attempt at setting up a clear boundary in Scotland between the lands under control of the Empire and those that were not. Reasons have been given for withdrawal from this series of forts, and later the Antonine Wall, that rely on events in other parts of the Empire. The idea has even been mooted that the tribes of the north were too 'primitive' to be conquered by the Romans! The Glory that was Rome? The Glamour that was Rome, more like – in the sense that modern scholars remain entranced or stupefied by the Romans.

After this retreat, there were several more invasions by the Romans, but each time they seem to have come up from their bases in England on a season-long campaign then gone back again. In the year 120CE, they proceeded to build Hadrian's Wall. Now, much has been made of the supposed fact that this structure must have meant that the tribes to the north of it would be under the influence of the great Roman Empire. Well, let's see. Hadrian's Wall[3] was built of stone from Wallsend on the Tyne to the River Irthing and was generally three metres wide and five to six metres high. From there to the west coast at Bowness-on-Solway, it was mainly built of turf, measuring six metres wide and three-and-a-half metres high. To the north, there was a ditch about six metres wide and three deep, with a bank on either side two metres high and set off about nine metres. This was a serious endeavour and suggests that there was a perceived need to stop tribal warriors from the north from coming south. It was also clearly a statement of Imperial might, and in itself a piece of propaganda. Look what we can do, you barbarians!

North of this, there are a considerable number of Roman forts. If, however, you look at them on a map they do not cover a substantial area and in fact follow the lines of repeated campaigns, and can be seen as effectively defending the supply lines for these campaigns, as well as for the Antonine Wall. This wall was raised c.142CE and abandoned c.165CE and there is evidence that it was not manned continuously through this period. Despite centuries of investigation, none of the forts show any nearby level of settlement by the incomers and it seems fair to describe all of the Roman presence in Scotland as military, though the chances are that there would have been some level of trading going on sporadically. During the four centuries that most the southern half of the island was an integral part of the Roman Empire, Scotland remained at best, from a Roman perspective, frontier country. It should also be remembered that south of Hadrian's Wall, the Romans had to deal with various 'rebellions', though I find it difficult to accept that people attempting to throw off the imposed military authority of an invading foreign power are rebelling. They are resisting, since the idea that they are rebelling suggests that there is some level of acceptability in their having been conquered. This is certainly acceptable, from the Roman point of view. It is also interesting, in terms of the persistent notion of some level of matriliny amongst the Pictish tribes north of Hadrian's Wall[4] that at least two of these uprisings were led by females: Boudicca and Cartimandua.[5]

A great deal has been made by various writers over the years of the fact that Roman coins, pottery and a hoard of Roman silver dating from a period of a couple of hundred years was found on Traprain Law. This in itself proves nothing, as it may all have been a result of a raid – as Dio Cassio said, 'they are fond of plundering'[6] – or even the result of a bartering process. In no way does

The hoard of Roman silver found at Traprain Law

63

it prove a client relationship with the Romans. While we cannot absolutely rule out some kind of temporary arrangement between native peoples and the incomers throughout 400 years, there is nothing to prove that this happened. Other than wishful thinking, that is. The Romans certainly invaded the northern half of Britain several times in the 1st and 2nd centuries CE, and in the early years of the 3rd century. An even later invasion took place at the beginning of the 4th century. The point is that they were invading, not occupying, and the fact that they had to keep on invading makes it quite obvious that they had no real control over any part of what is now Scotland, other than perhaps the few years that the Antonine Wall was continuously manned. That wall, like the bases at Cramond, Inversek on the Forth and Old Kilpatrick on the Clyde, may well have been supplied much of the time by sea, given that the Antonine Wall runs from the Forth to the Clyde (or vice-versa), and both rivers were probably navigable for supply ships at the time. Further north, the fort of Carpow, built where the Earn enters the Tay, could similarly have been supplied by sea, and though there is some evidence of Pictish shipping, there is little doubt that the Roman navy ruled the seas.

Everywhere the Romans went in Scotland, they built forts and marching camps. It seems that they needed to defend themselves whenever they were in this part of the world. We know that Scotland was tribal at the time and that there were no centres of political power akin to the Roman cities. It is noticeable, however, that many Roman forts and camps are in close proximity to hills that seem to have had considerable importance in tribal society, such as Edinburgh Castle Rock, the Eildons, Loudon Hill, etc., but these locales have never been proven to have been the permanent residences of any political elites. I have suggested elsewhere that the militaristic interpretation of every hill-top structure in Scotland as a fort is a misreading of sites, which were often in fact the locations for a range of tribal/communal activities.[7] The

Eildon Hills

preferred method of conquest for the Romans was to take over an already centralised society and effectively replace the elite structure with their own people, who could organise the raising of taxes. Tribalism is formed around kin relationships and does have elites, but they are not separate from the community as a whole. Therefore, the Romans could not simply annex already structured hierarchies and seem also to have had considerable trouble in battle with the natives, Caledonians, Picts, Maetae, Votadini, or whatever term was being currently used. In fact, Dio Cassius is on record as saying that they had lost 50,000 men in Scotland. He was writing in the early years of the 3rd century, which suggests that the various invasions up until then had met a great deal of resistance. Not a good basis for any 'client relationship'.

That resistance is mentioned in detail only once, the Battle of Mons Graupius, for which, of course, we only have one Roman source, and that was written by the son-in-law of the Roman general involved. Given the Christian-Classical bias of our education system over so many centuries, it is perhaps no surprise that the search for the location of this putative battle has been the subject of so much speculation. Andrew Breeze suggested that the name Graupius itself may be related to the Welsh word *Crib*, meaning ridge – the Picts probably spoke an Archaic Brythonnic dialect – and suggests, on geological grounds, that this refers to Bennachie in Aberdeenshire.[8] I would suggest an ever more striking ridge, like the one between the Lomond Hills in Fife that, like Bennachie, also show many markers of having been the site of ritual, community activities.[9] However, another point about Mons Graupius is that it is the only actual pitched battle recorded as having taken place between the northern tribes and the invading Romans in almost 400 years. This is of considerable significance. It may in fact be the case that the Caledonian tribes, lured into such a pitched battle by the invaders, learned the lesson and in future utilised the small-scale raiding techniques they had developed since the Iron Age. Dio Cassio hints at ambush tactics when he tells us:

> They can endure hunger and cold and any kind of hardship; for they plunge into the swamps and exist there for many days with only their heads above water, and in the forests they support themselves upon bark and roots, and for all emergencies they prepare a certain kind of food, the eating of a small portion of which, the size of a bean, prevents them from feeling either hunger or thirst.[10]

If this assumption is correct and the northern British tribes continued to fight quasi-guerrilla actions against the Romans, this could account for the repeated failure of the invasions themselves. There were no capitals or political centres the Romans could take over, and thus subdue the natives. Yet, they kept trying. An analogy might be the recent debacles of the British, and latterly the Americans – and their camp-followers in Afghanistan. Thousands of lives and countless treasure has been spent and lost – to what effect?

The main problem we have, of course, is that the mindset of Received Opinion is that the Romans were 'a good thing'. More than that, of course, England itself was part of the Roman Empire for four centuries. It is in important part of English history. The same does not apply to Scotland, and it never has. Julius Caesar may have come, seen and conquered the southern half of the island, but his successors never managed the same thing in the north. This mindset is still in existence. There are still those, claiming to be historians, who repeat the old chestnut that the Picts were so-called by the Romans because they tattooed themselves. This ignorance is astonishing, if, sadly, not surprising. Such lazy repetition of unsubstantiated ideas ignores the reality that many Roman soldiers were themselves tattooed, so why would they call a whole series of tribes after this habit? There is also the fact that a pair of Roman specialists, writing many years ago, explained the probable origin of the term as a native tribal name.[11]

The adherence to this idea that the Romans must have had some degree of control over the southern half of Scotland affects all sorts of things. Over the past couple of decades, there has been a great revival of interest in the Scottish provenance of cultural references to 'King' Arthur. Some insist in trying to explain him as some kind of hangover from a Romanised period of our history, an explanation that, frankly, cannot be supported by any evidence whatsoever. Much is made of Welsh genealogies, dating from much later, in which certain early figures are said to have had Roman, or at least Romanised, predecessors. One such, Cunedda, a putative 5th-century Briton from southern Scotland, is said to have been descended from Aetern, Padern and Tacit, which are read as the Roman names Eternus, Paternus and Tacitus. Given the Roman influence on Western scholarship and the fact that so much of our early written material emanates from within Christian enclaves, and is written in Latin, it is hardly surprising that written name-forms correspond to the education of the scribes themselves. Some historians assume that Paternus worked for the Romans, purely because he is referred to as *Pesrut*, meaning 'red cloak', and apparently suggesting this must have been given him by the Romans because they wore red cloaks. This is a trifle too speculative even for my taste.[12] Beyond this, it is taken as 'proof' that they must have been in a client relationship with the Romans. I am reminded of the numerous Hollywood instances of Native American warriors wearing the jackets of American soldiers, taken from the dead in battle. I believe it is difficult to overstate the influence of the Classical-Christian scholarly mindset and think it must lead to a necessary forensic approach to our early written sources. Would anyone suggest that the thousands of African-Americans with Scottish surnames took them out of respect for the slave-owners who had raped their female ancestors, rather than because it was administratively convenient for them to be registered as having such names when freed?

Notes

1   Tacitus; *On Britain and Germany*; Penguin; London; 1948. p. 79f.

2   www.theromangaskproject.org.uk/

3   www.aboutscotland.co.uk/hadrian/

4   Gray, KA; 'A New Look at the Pictish King List', in *Pictish Arts Society Journal*, issue 10; Edinburgh; 1996. See also Gray, KA; 'Matriliny at the Millennium: the Question of Pictish Matrilineal Succession Revisited' in *Pictish Arts Society Journal*, Vol. 14; Edinburgh 1999. pp. 13–32.

5   womenshistory.about.com/od/boudicca/p/boudicca.html
www.archaeology.wyjs.org.uk/romanweb/Cartimandua.html

6   Dio Cassius; *Dio's Roman History*, trans. by E. Cary; Heinemann; London; 1927. p. 246.

7   McHardy SA; *The Quest for the Nine Maidens*; Luath; Edinburgh; 2003. pp. 46–7.

8   Breeze, A; 'Philology on Tacitus's Graupian Hill and Trucculan Harbour', in *Proceedings of Society of Antiquaries of Scotland*, issue 132; 2002. p. 305ff.

9   McHardy, SA; *The Pagan Symbols of the Picts*; Luath; Edinburgh; 2012. p. 126.

10 Dio Cassius; *Dio's Roman History*, p. 246. The 'certain kind of food' is probably the Kale Pea: see Moffat, B; 'A Marvellous Plant', in *Folio*, issue 1; National Library of Scotland; Edinburgh; 2000. pp. 13–15.

11 Rivet, A and Smith, C; *The Place-Names of Roman Britain*; Batsford Ltd; London; 1979. p. 478.

12 Clarkson, T; *The Men of the North*; John Donald; Edinburgh; 2010. p. 22.

CHAPTER FIVE

Spinning the Scots

IN THE MAGAZINE *Antiquity* in the year 2000, Ewan Campbell of Glasgow University had an article entitled *Were the Scots Irish?*[1] In it he looked at the evidence for that cornerstone of Scottish history, the arrival of the Scots from Ulster into Argyll in the 6th century. He looked for contemporary historical, archaeological and linguistic evidence for this arrival and found... none. The first 'historical' reference to this supposed event comes from Bede writing over 200 years later[2] and there is no archaeological evidence to support the idea. This is of considerable importance in understanding the actual history of Scotland, as it has been part of Received Opinion for over a millennium. The subtext of this ongoing interpretation of our past is that we, as Scots, are originally Irish. It would be utter folly to deny the close cultural and political interactions between Scotland and Ireland going back into deep prehistory, but the idea that our nation's name originated with a set of tribes who only arrived here a millennium-and-a-half ago is, as Campbell's article clearly shows, something that appears to have no basis in fact. Cultural interaction with the Irish is something that has continued into modern times, and though I find the concept of pan-Celticism dangerously close to a form of racism, I am perfectly aware that my own antecedents contain two great-grandparents from Donegal. Like all humans I am a mongrel, and proud of it.

There are two specific aspects of rejecting this idea of the Scots invading from Ulster (though no doubt some of the original settlers after the Ice Age may well have followed such a route north) to found Dalriada that are, I would suggest, of considerable importance. The first is that if the Scots are as indigenous to Argyll and the Inner Hebrides as the Picts are to eastern and northern Scotland, which is what Campbell's article suggests, we have to reconsider how we treat our prehistory and early history. Instead of focusing on the supposedly important date of 500CE and what appears to be a non-existent immigration, we should be looking to see what evidence there is that tells of co-operation between the tribes of the east and west. Just how close were their socio-economic structures? Did they have the same primal religion? How much trade, inter-marriage and social intercourse was there between them? Of course, this needs some kind of cohesive and organised structure for future Scottish archaeology, but in the current climate it is something that I am sure would find a considerable amount of public support. The second interesting aspect is, if there is no evidence of such an invasion, why and how did the story arise?

I have suggested elsewhere that the Scots apparently being as indigenous as the other Caledonian tribes means that their working hand-in-glove with the Picts to attack the Romans early on suggests an ongoing, sophisticated inter-relationship between these peoples. This may well have gone back a long time before the so-called 'Barbarian Conspiracy' of 360CE, which saw them overwhelm Hadrian's Wall. The effect of the notion of Irish origin on our history has been to overemphasise the differences between the Picts and Scots, particularly by concentrating on the most obvious difference between them: language. What language the Picts spoke is still somewhat unclear, though it is generally accepted that they spoke some form of P-Celtic, as opposed to the Q-Celtic Gaelic of the Scots. Given that our understanding of the far past is no longer slavishly attached to the elite notion of invaders, we cannot be sure how long the Celtic languages have actually been spoken in Scotland. It is even within the bounds of possibility that these languages, and their variants, have been spoken here for millennia. With the necessary re-adjustment of our understanding of the past arising from the recent Orkney discoveries, is it conceivable that the split between Q- and P-Celtic actually happened here? Another possibility raised by EWB Nicholson was that Pictish was closer to Gaelic that the other Brythonnic dialects spoken in the 1st millennium by the Britons of Strathclyde, the Gododdin and the Welsh.[3] Recent ideas concerning the eventual joining together of the Picts and Scots lean more towards amalgamation rather than any kind of conquest, and this may have been seen as a natural development at the time.

Dalriada was, and is, different geographically from the southern and eastern parts of the country. The west of Scotland, with its sea lochs and high mountains, is much more like Norway than the east of Scotland, a fact that was of considerable significance when the Norsemen came to settle here. What this meant since very early times was that the best way of communicating was by boat. The old joke about the Hebridean and the Jew is worth repeating – they meet up on the Continent and the Jew says that his people are the oldest on the planet, having been the only people to have survived the Flood. 'Aye right,' says the Hebridean, 'and when did you ever hear of a Skyeman that didn't have his own boat'.

Traditional stories and oral culture have the capacity to retain ideas and data over considerable lengths of time, and have much to teach us about our past. The underlying point here is that we do not need outsiders' histories to tell us who we are. This sea communication was necessitated precisely by the landscape and may well have given rise to a much more centralised form of social structure in the west than in the east. The *Senchus Fer n Alban*, an Irish document that survives from the 14th century, but which refers back to Argyll in the 10th and possibly the 7th century, spells out the military obligations of the three constituent peoples or tribes of Dalriada – the Cenél nGabráin, the Cenél Loairn, and the Cenél nOengusa.[4] It is quite obvious that here we see three tribal peoples that are named after individuals in a similar fashion to the later Scottish clans. The *Senchus* makes mention of the number of men needed to man a *birlinn*, the favoured vessel of the Dalriadans. This suggests that the role of these vessels was central to the warrior culture of the time. Given that we know there was regular contact with Ulster – and Campbell suggests that the dominant influence was from Dalriada to Northern Ireland – we can consider Dalriada to have been a kind of thallassocracy (a sea-based polity or society). This would have meant that communications were probably more highly developed than in other parts of Scotland, which were to a great extent covered with vegetation and bog. This further suggests a greater cohesion and even centralisation of Dalriadan society than elsewhere amongst the tribes of the northern half of the British Isles in the 1st millennium. This, combined with the shared culture of the Q-Celtic languages, may well have made Dalriada particularly attractive to the evangelising Columba when he did turn up from Ireland in 563CE.

He had effectively been exiled from Ireland after starting a feud with his behaviour over a copy of a Psalter owned by St Finnan. He had been found guilty of theft and resisted the judgement by calling out his own clan, and a battle was fought at Cul Dreibhne in 561CE. He barely escaped excommunication and arrived in Scotland with the plan of supposedly converting as many non-believers as Christians had died in the battle. Most of what we think we know about Columba comes from the *Life of the Saint,* written by his successor Adomnan towards the end of the 7th century. He tells us that Columba became directly involved in the selection of the King Aidan MacGabhran in the 570s. What Adomnan does not mention is the story of the Scots having preceded Columba into Scotland a few generations before. By his own actions, Columba can be understood as someone who was deeply involved in political behaviour, and his role as the eventual patron saint of Scotland has tended to overshadow this. After his own Columban church was superseded by the Church of Rome, following the Synod of Whitby in 664CE, he was taken over by them as a figurehead, his monastery on Iona becoming a place of pilgrimage that lasts to this day. Adomnan, who appears to have been happy to accept the authority of Rome, may well have been involved in this process. What is clear is that with the takeover of the various Columban churches in Scotland and Ireland, the lands that they farmed and lived on became the property of the Church of Rome. The previous relationship between the Columban church and local society is not absolutely clear, but given the nature of society in northern Britain at the time it must have included some sort of accommodation with tribalism, with Columba himself being originally one of the O'Neill clan in Ireland. Did the land that the Columban church occupied still form part of the essentially communal tribal lands?

What Columba's behaviour and the political machinations at and after the Synod Whitby clearly show is a church that is considerably more than spiritual. There are some grounds for supposing that at this period the church militant may have had a strong role in what is now Scotland, but there is an aspect to the telling of history that is always propagandistic, especially when the sources being relied on are written by clerics whose first loyalty is to their God and their church. If the Christianisation of the country did involve bloodshed, as it certainly has in other places at other times, then we would not expect the Church to tell us about it and, of course, all our early 'historical' documentation was written by monks. The devotion to the Christian 'message' may help explain why the story of the Scots coming into Scotland a few generations before Columba arose.

There are reports of earlier Christian missionaries in Scotland

– St Ninian at Whithorn, Merchard and Fergus in the north – but Columba has become the dominant figure, the hero who Christianised Scotland. One of the problems any new religion faces is how to deal with the established ritual behaviour and beliefs of the indigenous population. There had been sophisticated ritual activity in Scotland for millennia before the arrival of Christianity. We do know is that it was deliberate policy in Bede's time to 'take over the pagan precincts', as Bishop Mellitus was told by Pope Gregory.[5] This is standard behaviour at any religious changeover – re-using sites where people have already been conducting their rituals makes sense on all sorts of levels. This is probably why so many early Church sites in Scotland and elsewhere are on raised mounds. These mounds had already been the sites of ritual activities, though they probably included as many social activities as purely religious ones. We have to be careful in describing ritual behaviour as religious when we have no clear idea of the specific beliefs of the participants. However, taking over a site and building a church on it would hardly have been enough around Dunadd, the capital of Dalriada, and quite probably where Aedan Mac Gabhran was based. Its site is in the river plain of the Add, from which it takes its name. Nowadays, this area is better known as Kilmartin Glen and it is one of the most complex sacred landscapes in Europe. Its great megalithic structures, cairns, stone circles and alignments are complemented by dozens of rock art sites in the area, some of which are still uncharted. This speaks of an area that had been used ritually for a very long time, and the dates for the stone circles at Temple Wood are roughly contemporaneous with activities at Ness of Brodgar, around 3000BCE. The rock art, mainly cup and ring carvings, is difficult to date but at least some of it may be earlier than even this. We know that there were people in the Kilmartin area as far back as at least 7000BCE, and perhaps even earlier. This is hardly an inconspicuous site and the wholesale destruction of all the various 'pagan'

Kilmartin sites may well have been beyond the powers of the new church, or perceived of as too provocative for the native population. If the Scots were indigenous to Argyll, they would have been the custodians of the ritual sites that abound in the area, even if there had been changes in how they were perceived and used over the thousands of years since their creation. Dougie Scott has pointed out that some of the Pictish Symbol Stones are re-used from much earlier times,[6] and there is no evidence to suggest that such a re-use of sites and artefacts associated with the ancestors is an uncommon human trait. It is what the Christians themselves were doing.

So how to deal with this site? The Christian church had one particularly effective new weapon in its battle with the old ways, which was unavailable to the followers of the primal religion – this was, of course, literature. Not just in terms of the supposed holy word of Scripture, but the actual process of writing things down. Within Christianity, the Book obviously held pride of place, but all of the educated monks were raised with a great respect for their education. The ongoing influence of Classical writing and thinking to this day underlines this. So what better way for the new religion to deal with this particular problem than to come up with a new story? The culture of the people they were spreading their word among was an oral one, in which the role of story was fundamental. Now they could have a new story that had the advantage of being written down. I therefore put forward the possibility that some cleric came up with the idea of suggesting a recent incursion, of a new people from Ireland, so it could be claimed that whatever these great monuments were, there was no one around to tell what they were. Thus, the tradition bearers of the Scots of Argyll were taken out of history at a stroke and the idea of the Scots as Irish took over. This played into the developing myth of the great Columba, a myth that was actively fostered by the Catholic Church in the centuries after the Synod of Whitby in 664CE, when the Columban church itself began to go into decline. The fact that the Columban church appears to have subsisted along the same tribal lines as society meant that its surviving splinters were small, localised and easily sidelined, while the power of the mother church spread the story that no one had any idea of what the great stones at Kilmartin signified. The story of the Irish incursion can thus be seen as a means of destroying any remaining power the primal religion may have held. This could not have happened overnight. But the future history of the area would hopefully allow no possibility of knowledge surviving about the stones and their uses.

It would not have happened overnight, but as we know Bede doesn't start writing about this until the 8th century, this would have left plenty of time. This, of course, is utterly speculative, but it makes a certain kind of sense if we remember that the function of Christian writing was not to describe what the cultural and historical reality of the indigenous people was, but to push the word of God. Could it have been Adomnan, the biographer of the great Columba? Possibly, but if so, why is there no mention of it in his Life of the Saint? The fact that the early Christian scribes were primarily concerned with religion means that we cannot take their writings at face value when it come to trying to get a clear picture of the past. This is not a value judgement, but a recognition of reality. When you further factor in that our universities were originally set up by, and for, clerics, you can understand why the story stuck. We must try to sift out what has been the result of propaganda. While this version of reality was as much matter of mindset as deliberate propaganda, the needs of the church always came first.

The idea that the primal religion that existed in Scotland before the arrival of Christianity is in any way worthy of consideration is relatively recent. The establishment position is always 'don't rock the boat' and, given that there even some

Presbyterians who saw themselves as the natural successors to the Columban church, we should be alert to the problems of sources derived from religious practitioners, particularly when Scotland has been riven, before and since the Reformation, by particularly vicious Christian sectarianism, sadly surviving to this day.

The idea of the Scots arriving not long before Columba has had fundamental effects on how we see our past. We have already seen the effect that it has had on our understanding of potentially mythological material and, in terms of our relationship with England (which will be looked at in the chapter on the Wars of Wallace and Bruce), this bias may well have had a considerable effect. Was the suggestion that we took our name from a people born elsewhere responsible for the fact that the Picts were ignored for so long in our history? The facts would appear to be that the Picts and Scots fought together against Romans and Northumbrians long before they were united into Alba in the 10th century. This new story also had the effect of further enhancing the cult of Columba. It may well be that Christianisation of Scotland was in fact anything but peaceful, but suffice it to say here that Columba, the Dove of Christ has been a powerful image for a very long time.

Before leaving this topic, however, I should say that there does appear to be evidence that the Christian religion and whatever preceded it, which I have been referring to as the primal religion, co-existed peacefully, certainly for a time. On the Glamis Manse Pictish Symbol Stone, we see on one side pre-Christian symbols and on the other an ornate Christian Cross. However, that cross is itself surrounded by symbols, some of which clearly seem to be referring to beliefs which were associated with rituals that had gone on in the pre-Christian period.[7]

Just as we rely on Christian scribes for the story of the Scots coming in from Ulster circa 500CE, so our understanding of the Vikings is essentially predicated on reports of attacks on Christian monasteries. This is in no way to suggest that such attacks did not take place, but as we know the Vikings were great traders as well as great raiders, we are entitled to ask if we have the complete picture. It is entirely understandable that Christian scribes would be horrified at the arrival of these raiders – they were pagans and as such were the enemy!

Given the spread of megalithic culture and the still extant contacts between Scotland and Scandinavia, it seems at least possible, if not likely, that contact over the North Sea and round the north of Scotland has been going on regularly since the Ice Age. One natural sea route would be from Norway via the northern isles and round to the Outer Hebrides, which is of course part of the area where the Norseman began to settle. We should not forget that the great Viking journey to settle in Iceland appears to have taken place from within the cultural area that included the west of Scotland and the east of Ireland. Within this area, the Gall-Gael culture developed. Henderson makes the point that the term 'Viking' itself is used earlier than the 8th century and not specifically used of raiders.[8] And, in later medieval times, the northern part of that area became the heartland of the Lordship of the Isles, which in time, like Galloway, the Borders and the Highlands, had to be brought into the Scottish nation through force. So, I think we are entitled to ask: how far back does that thallassocratic society go? And how far had some of those present at the Ness of Brodgar feast for closing down the temple come?[9]

Notes

1   Campbell, E; 'Were the Scots Irish?' in *Antiquity*; 2000.
    www.electricscotland.com/history/articles/scotsirish.html
2   Bede; *A History of the English Church and People*; Penguin; London; 1955. p. 39.
3   Nicholson, EWB; *Keltic Researches*; Oxford University Press; London; 1904. p. 1.

4   clanmaclochlainn.com/shenchus.html
5   Bede, *op cit*, p. 86.
6   Scott, D; *Watchers of the Dawn* (CD-Rom); Tain; 2001.
7   McHardy, SA; *The Pagan Symbols of the Picts*; Luath; Edinburgh; 2011. p. 153.
8   Henderson, G; *The Norse Influence on Celtic Scotland*; MacMillan; London; 1910. p. 12.
9   http://www.orkneyjar.com/archaeology/nessofbrodgar/ excavation-background-2/a-millennium-of-activity/

CHAPTER SIX

What War of Independence?

ONE OF THE clearest distortions in Scottish history is the use of the term 'Wars of Scottish Independence'. This has long been the term used to describe the battles between the Scottish people, and Kings Edward I and II of England. The role of William Wallace alone shows that this was more than just a dynastic struggle between different aristocrats. Wallace has been presented as leading a resistance movement that the nobles only later rallied comprehensively behind. While we are in the situation of being forced to rely on very little hard evidence for Wallace's activities, the survival of Blind Harry's epic poem has served as a bedrock

of what many Scots believed happened. The fact that English invasions of Scotland continued for centuries after this is something that cannot be denied, and the need to resist invasion from the south was a constant problem for the Scottish people in the southern parts of the country.

The underlying reality is that Scotland can be seen as a nation state before England was, with most commentators seeing the amalgamation of the Dalriadic and Pictish areas in the 9th century as the true

Statue of William Wallace, Scottish Borders

beginnings of Scotland. It was a couple of generations later that the Kings of Wessex began to claim the title of Kings of England, and considerably later that their descendants managed to establish their rule of the whole of what we call England. Similarly, of course, Scotland only attained its present shape in the late Middle Ages with the passing of the last remnants of Norse power in the northern mainland, Orkney and Shetland, in 1470. But why have we allowed ourselves to be led into a position where an absolutely central part of our history has been designated in such a way as to fundamentally undermine what this history tells us? For the point about the closing years of the 13th century and what followed was that it was a battle for survival by the Scots against a southern invader set on military conquest, no less than the Romans had been a millennium earlier. The truth is that the subtext of the term 'Wars of Scottish Independence' is that Scotland's natural role is to be part of Britain and, not only that, but a Britain in which the dominant force is, naturally, England. That this terminology has been so blindly accepted by generations of professional historians in Scotland is a matter for some reflection. The period itself, however, has much to teach us about the history process itself.

The claim of Edward I of England on Scotland was a result of political intrigue and deliberate dishonesty. In 1286, Scotland was plunged into crisis by the sudden death of Alexander III. His closest living relative was Margaret, the Maid of Norway, daughter of Eric II of Norway and Alexander's own daughter, also Margaret. She was an infant, so the immediate care of the kingdom was put in the hands of nine Guardians. This was necessary, as there were several families with competing claims to the Scottish throne and civil war was a distinct possibility. Her Guardians were the bishops of St Andrews and Dunkeld, plus four representatives of leading families. Significantly, the Guardians presented themselves as 'appointed by common counsel and

WHAT WAR OF INDEPENDENCE?

elected by the community of the realm'. Many historians like to present what happened during subsequent decades as being centred round the doctrine of feudalism, but we might obtain a better picture by looking at the great families as the direct successors of earlier tribal leaders, much as clan chiefs were. With the growth of the nation state, it was generally perceived that strong central-ised government was needed, by kings and others at the centre themselves. Their control of history has ensured that it is accepted teaching in all history that a strong centralised authority is 'a good thing'. People living far from the centre of power, and thus usually deprived of influence even over their own lives, would perhaps not agree. This matters because the centralisation of power has meant that questions about land use and land ownership have remain unresolved for so long. It is obscene that cash is the only criterion for owning Scottish land – does anyone think these circumstances would exist without the support of the centralised state and those who control it?

As early as 1286, it seems the Guardians approached Edward I for advice as to how to ensure stability and succession. This seems not unreasonable, as Edward was the Christian monarch of a neighbouring kingdom, sharing a considerable extent of cultural and religious aspects of society. Religion, however, though often a handy excuse for a range of activities by despots, has rarely if ever exercised any actual moral or political authority over elites. Alexander III, when he gave homage to Edward at Westminster in October 1278, said, 'I become your man for the lands which I hold of you in the kingdom of England for which I owe homage, saving my kingdom'. He then went on, 'No one has right to homage for my kingdom of Scotland save God alone, and I hold it only of God'. Edward had plans of his own. These plans were complex and well thought through, and the aim was complete control of the island of Britain for himself and his heirs. However, the Guardians were initially successful in keeping the (relative) peace and defending the realm. Some of the worst trouble was in the southwest in 1286, where the Bruces came close to open revolt.

There are two aspects of what happened next that have to be understood. One, the manipulation of feudal doctrine, and two, the deliberate distortion of history to bolster Edward's expansionism. Edward was trying consistently, from the 1270s onwards, to turn his feudal overlordship over the Scottish king and various nobles for lands in England into an outright and absolute claim over the whole of Scotland. This involved the use of spurious history, as well as the use of naked force and the destruction and theft of much of the literary material that was extant in contemporary Scotland.

In 1290, the Maid of Norway died and the worst-case scenario unfolded. Four major claimants came forward. They were John Hastings of Abergevenny in Wales; Florence V, Count of Holland; John Balliol of Galloway; and Robert Bruce, Earl of Annandale, grandfather of the eventual King Robert I. All claimed descent from Henry, son of David I King of Scots 1124–53, who had consolidated royal power over central Scotland, at least. All of them held various lands in Scotland and England but Bruce and Balliol were born and based here. Edward I was asked to help adjudicate the question and Balliol's claim was overwhelmingly approved in 1291 at Norham, significantly on the English side of the border. During the process, Edward took every opportunity to stress his feudal superiority over the claimants for lands in England despite the Treaty of Brigham 1290, in which he had promised to uphold the laws and customs of Scotland. Balliol did accept Edward's superiority, an act which was to cost Scotland dearly. Edward made much of what he saw as his own rights, always claiming legality, but forgetting the oaths he had earlier given.

In all this, Edward's strategy is clear. He was using feudal obligations to try and take over a separate kingdom – something no feudal monarch had ever tried to do before. He was, in fact, putting feudal obligations before the law of the land – at least as far as Scotland is concerned, despite his sacred oath to observe Scotland's laws and customs. While feudalism in Scotland was never much more than skin deep, there can be no doubt at all that landholders like Bruce and Balliol did owe some allegiance to Edward – for their English holdings alone. The problem we face today is that so many historians keep on referring to Scotland as a feudal country at this time. While there is no doubt that David I, raised at the English court, had brought some Norman Knights with him when he acceded to the throne in 1124, the extent of the Normanisation of Scotland is open to question. Feudal practices appear to have been the norm at David I's court and many land charters using feudal language were given out. However, we must remember that vast areas of Scotland – Galloway, the Borders, the Highlands and Islands – were not effectively brought under any form of centralised authority for centuries. But there was a second strand to Edward's strategy: the historical one.

In order to bolster his legally non-existent claims to Scotland, Edward had decided to show the Scots, or more likely his fellow European monarchs and the Pope, that he did have an ancient claim to the whole of Britain. All monarchs, just like modern governments of the most repressive kinds, always want to present a veneer of respectability. After all, if Edward was simply taking Scotland by force, he could do the same thing with parts of mainland Europe – the ongoing battles between France and England lasted for another half millennium after his death. He seized upon a claim that the Britons were descended from Brutus, a Trojan who had come and conquered all of Britain immediately after the Trojan War. This theory had been put forward by Geoffrey of Monmouth in his *Historia Regum Britanniae* (*The History of the Kings of Britain*), written in the mid-12th century and, in Medieval terms, a bestseller. This is a fascinating compilation of history, tradition and what appears to be pure fantasy. But what Geoffrey was doing with the story of Brutus the Trojan ruling the whole of the Island of Britain is obvious. He was creating a history for his time that conformed to the mindset of Classical Christian education, and to the political needs of his audience, the Anglo-Norman ruling class of England. By referring back to such a distant period of the past, he was legitimising contemporary political reality. No one who read Geoffrey, amongst the limited numbers of literate people at the time, was likely to have had a different mindset. As William Ferguson pointed out, Geoffrey went further, claiming that Brutus lived at same time as the Biblical prophet Samuel.[1] It is interesting that Geoffrey was also the one to bring King Arthur to the fore, a figure who served as a model for several kings in their attempts to unite the island. However, it should be remembered that despite centuries of interpretation of the figure of Arthur as Welsh, Cornish, or even English, the first dateable reference to him occurs in the poem *Y Gododdin*, written in Edinburgh c. 600CE.[2] Arthur was as much a part of the P-Celtic speaking cultures of Scotland as Wales and elsewhere.

Using Geoffrey's history to bolster his acquisitiveness was a clever move on Edward's part. He was claiming what was a historical right, a trick used by monarchs and politicians throughout the ages. The Scots, however, well aware that Scotland had never been a part of England, and not inclined to submit to a foreign king, were also literate and part of the Classical Christian tradition. So arose the need for a counterstory. This was the famous story of Scota, daughter of Pharaoh, which crops up in the 1320 Declaration of Arbroath:

> Most Holy Father and Lord, we know and from the chronicles and books of the ancients we find that among other famous nations our own, the Scots, has been graced with widespread renown. They journeyed from Greater Scythia

by way of the Tyrrhenian Sea and the Pillars of Hercules, and dwelt for a long course of time in Spain among the most savage tribes, but here could they be subdued by any race, however barbarous. Thence they came, twelve hundred years after the people of Israel crossed the Red Sea, to their home in the west where they still live today. The Britons they first drove out, the Picts they utterly destroyed, and, even though very often assailed by the Norwegians, the Danes and the English, they took possession of that home with many victories and untold efforts; and, as the historians of old time bear witness, they have held it free of all bondage ever since.[3]

The story of Scota, who had led this journey from 'Greater Scythia, was originally taken from an Irish source, the *Lebor Gabala Erenn*, the spin about the Scots originating in Ireland being very much a part of Scottish historical belief at the time. Written in the 11th century, *Lebor Gabala Erenn* (*The Book of Invasions of Ireland*) was an early attempt to create a history of Ireland that conformed to dominant ideas of the time. Unsurprisingly, the Bible, with its history of the Israelites, was a powerful influence. Its version of Irish history developed through waves of successive invaders. It may well be that within this work that there are remnants of past events that had been passed down through the oral tradition, even if the creation of such 'histories' was the work of monks steeped in the Classical Christian tradition. What is intriguing is that in the story, Scota and her followers are said to have come into Ireland from the Iberian Peninsula. As Stephen Oppenheimer pointed out, it was from a location in the north of Spain that the first settlers arrived in the British Isles after the last Ice Age.[4]

There is a clear need for a national history in all cultures. In pre-literate and tribal times, such histories are passed on orally, but once literature is present the need arises for any 'new' history to conform to what is already known and accepted within society.

And, in the case of societies where literacy is the preserve of people of a particular religious persuasion, history will always be shaped to conform to their values. And, when education is controlled by the same privileged group, history is clearly not an objective reality but essentially a political tool. In this respect, what is taught is of primary importance and it is no coincidence that it is only since the institution of the Scottish Parliament that Scottish history is officially part of the Curriculum for our children. Let us hope that those in charge of the Curriculum stop propagating the notion that Scotland ever was a part of England.

Notes

1   Ferguson, W; *The Identity of the Scottish Nation*; Edinburgh University Press; Edinburgh; 1998. p. 24.
2   Koch, JT; *The Gododdin of Aneurin*; University of Wales Press; Cardiff; 1997.
3   http://www.nas.gov.uk/downloads/declarationArbroath.pdf
4   Oppenheimer, S; *The Origins of the British: A Genetic Detective Story*; Constable and Robinson; London; 2006.

CHAPTER SEVEN

What's in a Name?

ONE OF THE reasons I am so loath to accept Received Opinion about descent from Normans is because of my own name. Most people would have no problem in recognising McHardy as a Gaelic (Celtic) name by the prefix Mc, alternatively Mac or M', all of which are Scots/English orthographical attempts to represent the original Gaelic for 'son of,' or 'of the tribe of'. Various interpretations of the second part of my surname have been given – one of which derives it from 'Caird' or tinker, once the high-status, travelling tin-smith from whom our modern-day and much-oppressed Travelling People are descended. However, I have come across an older, different genealogy that claims the name comes from a French equerry to the Dauphin, or Crown Prince of France, who along with David I was a hostage at the 12th-century English court.[1] Supposedly, David was impressed by this equerry when he stepped in to prevent an insult to his master by the English king. 'Toute hardi' (too rash), the Dauphin is supposed to have said, at which, quick as a flash, David quipped 'Il sera deshormais hardi' (he will be called Hardy from now on), and gave him lands at Corgarrf in Aberdeenshire. There is another story of our origin which is still told amongst both McHardies and Hardies in Scotland to this day.[2] The Hardies and McHardies seem to have originated around Corgarrf and Strathdon in Aberdeenshire. I was not told the story in my family, apparently because my great grandfather married a Catholic and changed religion. My father and his siblings were therefore brought up with the ridiculous idea that because our name is McHardy, not MacHardy, we were of Irish descent. I can only presume this was to do with religion. Strangely, however, my father was also told that we were of Viking descent, which turns out to be very interesting indeed. The story involves an archer who falls foul of the king and is forced to shoot a peat off his wife's head to save his life. On being asked by the king to join his bodyguard, he refuses and is deemed a 'hardy' fellow. The interesting thing about this is that it is very like the story of Orvandel from Norse myth[3] and there is at least one other notable McHardy archer in tradition.[4] There were also a group, or perhaps a tribe of people, living over in Norway called Hardison in the early Middle Ages, so, given the contact between the peoples of the British Isles and those of the North Sea littoral areas since Stone Age times, the idea of some Viking blood seems at least within the bounds of possibility. I am well aware of the Viking influence in Ireland, and from a DNA point of view, I may have some Viking in me from my ancestors from Donegal.

But names are interpreted to mean different things, and emphasise different origins, and the putative French origin conforms to what appears to be a long-established process in Scottish history. A great deal has been said in histories of Scotland about Scotland being a feudal country, just like England. We have charters written in classic feudal style to show it. All of this supposed feudalism started with an influx of Norman knights, said to have been brought into Scotland by David I (1124–1153) when he returned from the English court in 1124, having spent quite a few years as the guest of the English king, Henry I. Here it seems young Davie, who had been driven into exile when his uncle Donald III had become king of Scots in 1093, was quite taken with Anglo-Norman ways of doing things. It was only when his brother, Alexander I, who had succeeded Donald in 1107, himself died in 1124 that David returned to Scotland to become David I, King of Scots. David had the backing of the English king and he needed it, because there was another claimant for the throne: Alexander's son, Malcolm.

The modern abject sycophancy of both media and politicians, and of all parties including the SNP, towards the current incumbent of the British throne is apparently based on some idea that the monarchy as an institution is good for society as a whole. Even the most superficial examination of the history of the monarchy in this island alone shows that blatant self-interest and bloodthirsty ruthlessness are the guiding principles of those intent on being a monarch. Things way well have calmed down since the 18th century but, in historical terms, that is relatively recent. One of the most important things about monarchy, of course, is that it legitimises the very idea of aristocracy, though the idea that anyone is born better than another is a psychotic delusion, born out of naked self-interest and perpetuated by privilege. It has no basis in objective reality, but then again as the Tea Party movement in America has recently shown, there are other kinds of argument.

As an example of this, David I handed out charters for vast areas of Scotland where it is patently obvious the King's law did not run. David was ultimately successful in stabilising his reign, but it took him ten years of hard fighting to make his position secure. In contemporary terms, it seems David saw himself as a moderniser – he instituted the Scottish burghs, he founded several monasteries and there is no doubt that he tried to institute feudalism. However, there is the rub. How successful was he? Just because something is written down does not make it fact. Much has been made of the fact that he brought many French and Anglo-Norman knights with him and granted them lands all across Scotland. This is said to be why there are so many 'mottes', or mounds, all over Scotland. The fact that most of these so-called 'mottes' are in fact prehistoric and seem to have been moot-hills, 'moot' meaning gathering, and the focus of all sorts of community activity is not itself too telling. For, after all, if these hordes of French knights had arrived, surely the mounds would have been just right for them to raise the castles or 'baileys' on. An assumption that this took place is hardly history. It has always struck me as a bit strange that a bailey is so like the Gaelic baile, meaning settlement, but what the heck. Received Opinion has it there were all these Norman knights ruling the pathetic Scottish peasantry and, of course, later generations of Scottish aristocrats have claimed descent from them. Well, that's where things tend to get a bit odd.

One thing we do know is that vast areas of Scotland remained essentially tribal until long after David's time. Before looking at more specific cases, there is one question that has to be answered. How do you take over a tribe? All the evidence from the Romans to the 18th century points to the kin-groups of the Highlands and the Borders as being societies in which at least the majority of adult males were trained in the use of weapons. The risible notion that battle was the preserve of some kind of tribal middle or upper class is totally contradicted by the numbers of men General Wade suggested could be raised in the Highlands as late as the 1720s – over 20,000. If this was some kind of 'aristocratic' section of the populace, it means that there must have been at least five to ten times that many 'non-aristocratic' males of fighting age, with the commensurate numbers of old men, children and women that this would suggest. Do the maths. Not every man had a full set of weapons in the Highlands, it was not a materially rich society, but when called to battle, all men of the clan responded. So how can you replace the leader of such an organisation, related as he is, in theory at least, to each and every one of these warriors? You cannot do it without destroying the very society you would be trying to take over. Certainly, if the situation fits it may be possible to marry into the ruling family of the clan, but how do you displace other candidates for the chiefship? That there was always at least a potential for some level of election to the position of chief is well-known. And there are even examples of already selected chiefs being deposed because they were not accepted as suitable by the clan as a whole.[5] The only way of taking over a tribe is to defeat them militarily with enough men to keep them subjugated. Evidence for this exists very sporadically, and in areas where it does appear to have happened, such as David I himself taking over Moray, it did not take long for the area to revert back to tribal mores.

Ever since David's time, there has been a consistent strand of Scottish thinking that emphasises Norman ancestry. Just as in the Received-Opinion notion of mottes being created all over the country, this needs to be tested. We can certainly see from David's time onwards that there are specific scribal habits that can give the impression of extensive Norman presence. Take David's nephew, whom he appointed to rule Moray after deposing Angus the Mormaor (chief or leader) of Moray. This nephew was William, who is referred to as William fitz Duncan. No one would argue that 'fitz' is not a Norman word, approximating to the Gaelic mac, but Duncan? He was the son of David's brother, Duncan, and by no stretch of the imagination can he be construed as a Norman. A would-be Norman? Possibly. Scribal conventions may apply? This may also suggest that others of David's companions may, likewise, not be as Norman as they seem.

Walter fitz Alan became the 'overlord' of extensive lands in Kyle. The Allan Water is a substantial river in Scotland's heartland and, as place-name scholars tell us, river names can be very old indeed. Another companion of David's was Hugh de Morville, which is an obvious Norman name. Ville is classic French, and though Mor is Gaelic for big, or great, there is undoubtedly a Morville in Normandy. He would certainly appear to be of Norman origin. And, of course, the prefix de is also French, n'est-ce pas? Aye, but. The use of scribal conventions is unarguable and it is telling that in Scottish usage 'the' has a particular relevance in names. The chiefs of Highland clans were known, in Scots and English as The MacDonald, The Macleod, The

Mackenzie, etc. This is precisely because their role as chief reflects the tribal reality that they represented the entire kin-group of their clan, as the supposedly closest living descendant of the person whose name the clan had adopted. I say adopted because the use of the patronymic (i.e. then name of the supposed founder of the clan) does not appear in widespread use before the Middle Ages. However, the practice was known much earlier, as we have already seen amongst the tribes of Dalriada. It is also a fact that in Scots usage, until very recently, it was the norm for farmers, tenants and owners to be referred to by society at large by the name of the farm on which they worked. A combination of these factors make it at least possible that much of the so-called Norman ancestry of our landowning class, whose primary interest is in holding onto their lands and privilege as much as in the Middle Ages, is somewhat suspect. I shall return to this.

Another question this led to is, if there had been such an extensive Norman takeover of Scotland, why are there so few Norman names on the Declaration of Arbroath? It is worth noting that the Declaration clearly stipulates that the assembled company, speaking on behalf of the Common Weal of Scotland (everybody), maintained the right to depose Robert I if he didn't keep the English out of Scotland. This is not a feudal procedure in any way, shape or form, and appears to me to be much more like the inherent right of the clan, through the Council of Elders, to remove the chief if he is acting against the interests of the community, as already noted. However, David I had instituted the fashion for all things French amongst those close to him and, given that some of the so-called Scottish nobility actually held lands in England, it would not be surprising if they conformed to the accepted idea of what an 'aristocrat' should be. How many French names do we actually have on the Declaration though? The following at first glance certainly appear to be French – William de Moravia, William II de Soules, John de Menteith,

Reproduction of the 'Tyninghame' (1320 AD) copy of the Declaration of Arbroath.

Gilbert de la Hay, Alexander de Lamberton, Thomas de Menzies, John de Inchmartin, and Thomas de Morham

Well Moravia is simply a Latinized version of Moray, Soules, Menteith, Inchmartin, Lamberton and Morham are Scottish place-names. De Umfraville certainly appears French. The question that surely has to be asked is this – did David I destroy enough of the traditional structures of Scottish kinship to be able to replace the existent heads of established, warrior-trained, kin-groups with new heads? The fact that almost 200 years later, the 1320

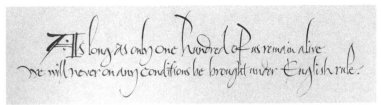

Detail from the 1320 Declaration of Arbroath

Declaration stipulates that the king is under the overall control of the people, designated as the Common Weal in the document itself, and reflecting kin-group behaviour suggests not.

In terms of the conventions of charter writing, I suggest that, time after time, Gaelic and Scots names were rendered into suitable Latinate forms. We know that long after David I's time that Galloway, the Borders – where de Soules was based – and the Highlands resisted centralized authority with a will. Those areas were still essentially tribal in the 13th century and it is of some importance to realise that the Douglases, who were such a thorn in the flesh to a succession of Stuart kings, had their power base in the Borders and, most importantly, among their own kin. An idea has been propagated that the Borders clans grew up as a result of the wars between Scotland and England. Yet, they were a warrior people who lived on specified territories and who were as addicted to raiding, mainly for cattle, as their cousins in the north were. Take away the fact that they did not speak Gaelic – they spoke Scots – and that they did not wear the tartan, and you can see they were in fact as kin-driven, territorial and warlike as the Highland clans. Given that there is no evidence to counter the idea all of Scotland was tribal until the middle of the 1st millennium, are we to think that the Borders moved from early tribalism into some other form of social structure, then back into what is clearly a tribal-type structure by the Middle Ages? It is a novel idea. Where is the evidence for it?

It seems to me that the various scribal conventions and aristocratic preferences mentioned, all start in David's time. That he was an admirer of feudalism's capacity to increase the power and wealth of centralised kingship is not in doubt. Nor is his apparent devotion to Christianity: he founded many monasteries, and it is from the monasteries that the scribes came. Not only were they dominated by what I have referred to as the Classical Christian mindset, they were also greatly beholden to David, who had given them so much. I think the eulogy written after his death by Ailred of Rievaulx, a Cistercian historian and close associate of the king, illustrates this very well:

> O desolate Scotia, who shall console thee? He is no more who made an untilled and barren land a land that is pleasant and plenteous, who adorned thee with castles and cities and lofty towers, enriched thy ports with foreign wares, gathered the wealth of other kingdoms for thine enjoyment, changed thy shaggy cloaks for precious raiment, clothed thine ancient nudity with purple and fine linen, ordered thy barbarous ways with Christian religion.[6]

The barbarous ways lasted a while yet.

Another possible example of the adoption of a French ancestry is de Comyn. The Comyns were heavily involved in the battle for succession at the end of the 13th century, one of them being killed in a church by Robert 1 and his henchmen. William de Comyn of Roxburgh was Chancellor of Scotland under David 1, but the name suggests a derivation other than Anglo-Norman. Apart from the fact that we have a Cummene, as an Abbot of Iona in 669CE, there is also the little matter of the clan badge of the Comyns or Cummings. The habit of having a clan plant to differentiate between the different clans – specific clan tartans do not appear to have a provenance much earlier than the 19th century – was common to all clans. The plant badge of the

Cummings is, of course, the cumin plant.[7] Are we supposed to believe that an incoming Norman knight, with the help of the king, wandered around Scotland until he found a clan that had as their badge a plant that bore his name? Those who want to believe otherwise will no doubt suggest that the plant badge arose after a foreigner arrived and took over the leadership of the local kin-group. Also, again, the Comyns are from a part of the Highlands, no matter what may have been written on a piece of vellum, that was well within the Gaeltadht, between Strathspey and the Great Glen and 'bandit country' until very late.

It is well known that the Campbells of Argyll, the most successful land-grabbers in Scottish history, actually have various genealogies – British, French, Irish and Norse. Having a genealogy for every occasion seems an excellent idea if you are going to protect your landholdings, no matter what comes to pass. However, it is not only great ducal families whose ancestry may be called into question.

The truth is that much of human activity and particularly charters, genealogies and other written materials so beloved of the historian, are all about land and, in Scottish terms, are about the move from communal to personal ownership. Most historical materials deal only with personal ownership. Why? *Cui buono?* The people who owned the land. These people who had the power could legitimise their own possessions, no matter how they had acquired them. Apart from monks, most of the population were illiterate in the Middle Ages, so if you could give a monastery a grant of land on your property you would have scribes on hand to provide you with charters, histories and genealogies. The possibilities such patronage raises are obvious.

One particular suggested Norman-derived name is of course de Bruce. This is from JA Mackay's *Robert the Bruce, King of Scotland* (1974):

Robert the Bruce statue, Bannockburn

the Bruces claimed a lineage which extended back to the Vikings in the far north. Traditionally they were descended from Lodver, the Norse Earl of Orkney who flourished in the tenth century. His son, the Earl Sigurt fell at the battle of Clontarf in 1014, when the Irish under Brian Boru routed the Vikings and broke their hold over eastern Ireland. Sigurt's second wife Olith... was a granddaughter of Malcolm IV, King of Scots, and from this marriage sprang Torphin, the progenitor of the Earls of Caithness. By an unnamed wife Sigurt produced four sons, Somerled, Brusee, Eyn and Whelp.[8]

Here we have the name Brusee, closely related to significant players in Scotland in the 11th century. The Anglo-Norman, feudal aristocratic Bruces are said to have originated in Normandy. Of course, the Normans were of Norse descent, but the general derivation of Bruce is that it comes from the name of a small village called Brix, near Cherbourg, in Normandy. It may be fortuitous then that their ancestral lands in Scotland were centred on Annandale – a name that our placename specialists assure us is a marker of Norse settlement, in the period *before* the Norman Conquest of England. You might think that it was a matter of some importance that the Bruces could show they were of French descent and therefore of just as high status as other contemporary leading families and rivals for the throne. The point is that there are other interpretations available – just as there seem to have been alternatives then.

Like the use of charters, historians have been all too ready to take at face value historical evidence that needs to be approached forensically. Yet again, the dead hand of Received Opinion has ensured this was not done. The need to approach such matters forensically (i.e. to test the validity of the evidence) arises precisely because of what accompanies these potentially forged genealogies, and the use of charters – the acquisition of land. Remember that Scotland has to this day the only totally open market in land in Europe – whoever you are, you can buy a bit of Scotland if you have the readies – and we can all see how much good that has done for the land, never mind the people.

Geoffrey Barrow, the leading Scottish feudal historian of the past half-century, made the point in his book about Robert the Bruce, 'The Scots, in short, were a kin-based society,' and this sits none too well with the hierarchic and rigid structure of what we think of as feudalism.[9] Barrow also tells us, 'In later ages it was common enough for men of all classes in Scotland, nobles, burghers and peasants, to address their sovereign with extra-ordinary bluntness'. Apart from neglecting to say how women might address the king, this sentence shows something else. In the phrase 'extraordinary bluntness', Barrow goes right to the heart of our Scottish historical dilemma. If it was 'common enough', how could it be 'extraordinary'? Well, it might be 'common enough' in Scotland, but it was certainly not the norm in England, nor I suspect in many other European countries. Here we have the nub of our problem – the commonplace in Scottish terms must be presented as anything but in 'British' terms. This should not surprise us. In terms of this island, most history is relatively recent – after all, a few centuries ago literacy was the exception, not the norm, even here in Scotland, where people sure seemed to like to read the Bible. Most of our history has been written after the Union of the Crowns (1603) and the Union of the Parliaments (1707). It therefore represents the interests and also the education of the ruling elite of the post-Union state. Is it not a sad indictment of those of supposedly higher status in Scottish society that they have so happily participated in creating a picture of Scotland that is built on external models, usually through reference to external sources and in ignorance of much of what happened – in Scotland?

And, within the clan system that survived into the middle of the 18th century, we have evidence that no matter how much Received Opinion insists the clans were feudal there is evidence to the contrary. This comes from Burt's *Letters of a Gentleman*, a collection of letters from the 1730s. He explains the Highlanders' relationship with their chief:

> [A]s the meanest among them pretend to be his Relations by Consanguinity, they insist upon the Privilege of taking him by the Hand whenever they meet him. Concerning this last, I once saw a Number of very discontented Countenances when a certain Lord, one of the Chiefs, endeavoured to evade this Ceremony. It was in Presence of an English Gentleman in high station, from whom he would have willingly have concealed the Knowledge of such seeming Familiarity with slaves of so wretched Appearance, and thinking it, I suppose, as a kind of Contradiction to what he had often boasted at other Times, viz., his despotic Power over his Clan.[10]

It is noticeable that he says that it is the member of the clan who insists upon his right to shake his Chief's hand. While this does not mean that the two were absolute equals, it does show that within the tribal/clan system there was a social system that was totally unlike that of England, where there were aristocracy, gentry and, effectively, serfs, or as Burt puts it here – slaves. There is a level of egalitarianism that not only contradicts, but has no obvious precursors in feudalism. The supposed absolute power of the Scottish chief over his clansmen does not fit in with this eye-witness account. The much-noted and scandalous situation on many Scottish Highland estates, even today, where the lairdie or landowner rules supreme, actually appears not to have developed from the time of the clans but from the growth of the Victorian shooting estate and the predominantly English notion of class amongst those developing such estates, no matter their country of origin.

That the adoption of what are effectively forged credentials has long been endemic has not passed entirely unnoticed. This from Allen, talking about the 17th century:

> Given the shamelessness with which even copper-bottomed aristocrats embellished their own genealogies, it should be no surprise that brazen arrivistes and nouveaux riches proved adept at fabricating for themselves antique credentials.[11]

Give the widespread manipulation of Scotland's story it is little wonder that such activities have been particularly rife here.

Notes

1   Laing, A; *The Donean Tourist*; J Booth; Aberdeen; 1828. p. 30.

2   Grant, J; *Legends of the Braes o Mar*; Alex Troup; Aberdeen; 1921. p. 10f.

3   Mackenzie, DA; *Teutonic Myth and Legend*; Harrap; London; 1912. p. 48.

4   MacConnochie, A; *Lochnagar*; Adelphi Press; Aberdeen; 1891. p. 127.

5   Scott, W; *Manners, Customs and History of the Highlands of Scotland*; Thomas Morison; Glasgow; 1893. p. 47. See also Burt, E; *Letters from the North of Scotland*; Birlinn; Edinburgh; 1998. p. xli.

6   www.algerclan.org/getperson.php?personID=I15347& tree=alger

7   Rennie, JA; *The Scottish People*; Hutchison; London; 1960. p. 117.

8   Mackay, JA; *Robert the Bruce, King of Scotland*; Robert Hale; London; 1974. p. 9.

9   Barrow, GWS, *Robert the Bruce and Scottish Identity*; Saltire Society; Edinburgh; 1984, p. 4.

10 Burt, *op cit*, p. 193.

11 Allen, D, 2002 *What's in a Name?: Pedigree and Propaganda in Seventeenth-Century Scotland*, as cited in Cowan, E & Finlay, RF *Scottish History; the Power of the Past*; Edinburgh University Press; Edinburgh.

CHAPTER EIGHT

After Charlie Left

THIS CHAPTER OFFERS a consideration of the evidence for the ongoing post-Culloden Jacobite resistance in Scotland and why it has been ignored.

In most histories of Scotland, the Battle of Culloden is presented as the swansong of Scottish Jacobitism. Recent years have seen a revival of interest in the *Lyon in Mourning*,[1] compiled between 1746 and 1775 by Robert Forbes, an Episcopal clergyman, which delineates the ethnic cleansing of the Scottish Highlands by the British Army – with several Scots prominent in the brutality – after the battle itself. Forbes compiled eyewitness accounts of the rapes, murders, theft of livestock, etc., which were part of the Duke of Cumberland's deliberate attempt to destroy the ancient Highland way of life once and for all, and which has led to the Duke still being known by many in Scotland as Butcher

An Incident in the Rebellion of 1745 (1746) by David Morier

Cumberland and the Union Jack still being referred to by some as the Butcher's Apron. There are many people, both south of the border and here in Scotland, who see any continuing interest in this period as being totally over the top and suggest that it is time that the Scots put such historical matters to rest. After all, it was a long time ago. The presentation of 'the whingeing Jock', forever going on about perceived injustices in the past, is one which constantly finds favour among the metrovincial commentariat of London and the Home Counties, but when history itself has been traduced, a bit of resentment is perhaps not unreasonable. And the history of the period has not been presented in its entirety.

For the truth of the matter is that the Jacobite cause did not die on Culloden Moor in 1746, and to understand why, we have to look at what the Jacobite cause in Scotland actually was. It is all too easy to portray it, as so many writers have done, as a doomed adventure in support of a romantic fool by a people whose society was anachronistic in the modern world; a mad last-gasp adventure of Iron Age throwbacks. However, just as the reality of what happened after Culloden tells a different story, so too can we interpret the actions of those who supported the Stuart cause from 1689 through to the 1750s in Scotland as being more than the adherence of benighted savages to the interests of a dynasty of buffoons. The portrayal of the '45 as being essentially a campaign by Gaelic-speaking Highlanders is simplistic, inaccurate and quite deliberate. No doubt Cumberland and his father George II, like so many Scottish kings in earlier centuries, were dead set on destroying the Highland warrior society of the Gael, but there was much more to it than that. That the ongoing existence of clan society, even as it was undergoing fundamental change, presented an almost permanent threat to centralised government, in Edinburgh or London, cannot be doubted. The clan system was a direct development from the society of Iron Age warrior tribes that had existed millennia earlier, and the warrior

The memorial cairn at the centre of the battlefield of Culloden,
near Inverness in Scotland

functions within such a society still held true. Even if chiefs had
been accepting the King's parchment as proof of their personal
ownership of lands for generations, lands that they and their
kinfolk had lived for generations before the Scottish state came
into existence, certain aspects of the original warrior system
remained. Even into the 18th century, the practice of inter-clan
raiding continued.[2] This was how the warriors and, in particular,
the potential chiefs showed their prowess. This inter-clan raiding,
common behaviour in pastoralist, tribal warrior societies across
the globe, meant that effectively every man in the clan, or tribe,
was trained in the use of arms. There is evidence to show that the
practice had a codified set of rules, and accepted patterns of

behaviour.[3] It is important to realise that the clans, like the tribes that had preceded them, were always ready to be involved in battle. However, the participants in the inter-clan raids and feuds which developed from them were not soldiers, they were warriors. They were interested in battle and glory, not in war and conquest, though by the 18th century, several of the clans, most particularly the Campbells, had moved far from the old ways and were expert at expanding their territory at the expense of other clans. The typical clan warrior was also bound by a code of honour that harked back to the mythical time of Finn MacCoul and the Fianna. This was *cothrom na Feinne*, the fair play of the Fianna, a system that was truly chivalric. However, the idea of having all men capable of bearing arms, even though not everyone could afford to own a full set of weapons, was also a defence mechanism. Through the use of the Crann Tara,[4] the Fiery Cross, the clans could summon virtually the entire adult male population to a predetermined spot within a matter of a few hours, armed and equipped either to act in defense of their own lands, or to go off and attack others. The specific martial traditions of the Highlands in effect meant that an army could be raised within hours, assembled and on the march before a Government army could even be planned. And, of course, the Highland charge was a tactic that had proved brutally effective on countless occasions, making the idea of a Highland host doubly fearsome.

The Jacobite army that existed in 1746 in fact contained more men from what we nowadays think of as the Lowlands, than Highland clansmen, but it was in the Highlands that the post-Culloden resistance continued. And it is also true that Bonnie Prince Charlie went out of his way to get uniforms based on Highland dress for the entire army, before they marched into England. In this we see the folly of youth, or perhaps the stupidity and arrogance of a royal, in that dressing his entire army as Highlanders played directly on the fears of the majority of the English

Prince Charles Edward Stuart, 1720–1788.
Eldest son of Prince James Francis Edward Stuart (1750) by William Mosman

population who had for centuries been led to believe they were nothing other than savages. To him they looked good, but the pathetic levels of recruitment to his cause once the Jacobite army was over the border may have been, at least in some part, the result of this particular choice on his part.

And it was due to ineptitude at the strategic level, and a personality clash between the Prince and Lord George Murray, his most efficient officer and effective military leader, that the campaign went severely wrong and culminated in the slaughter at Culloden. If ever there was a battle fought in the wrong place at the wrong time this was it, the leadership on the day contributing greatly to the crushing defeat. However, remembering that the Jacobites had previously defeated British armies in the battles at Prestonpans and Falkirk, there was no immediate perception that this was the end of the Jacobite cause. Several thousand Jacobite troops had not even been at Culloden, and even with the horrific casualties suffered on the field there were still a considerable number of troops on the Jacobite side. Or there would have been if Charlie hadn't given the order to disband a couple of days later. Not 'disband and keep yourselves in readiness', not 'disband and continue a campaign of harassment against the British Army', simply 'disband'. He then went on the run for several months in the Highlands, before escaping on a ship to France. For some of those left behind as the British Army tore through the Highlands in an orgy of looting, raping and murder (see the *The Lyon in Mourning* by Robert Forbes), there was no possibility of surrender. Many of the prisoners taken died in stinking prison hulks in the Thames, others went off to a life of slavery under the baking Jamaican sun, and many were executed. Of those who did not surrender, and this included men who had fought in the French Army against the British, so there would be no hope of any eventual amnesty, the only option was to flee abroad or fight on as best they could.

In various published works from the period, such as the Allardyce Papers,[5] and the Albemarle Papers,[6] the reader can find situation reports from British Army officers in garrisons in various parts of the Highlands. These date well into the 1750s. Interestingly a collection of these was included as an appendix to the 19th-century book, *Glasgow Past and Present*,[7] perhaps because somebody thought this material should be in print somewhere, but to date they have never been collected and published as a specific historical resource. The language in these situation reports is often telling. This is from Captain Johnstone at Invercomrie, 10 November 1752:

> It is a truth well known, that the inhabitants of Rannoch in general, but especially upon the estate of the late Strowan (Robertson), are notorious thieves. If there are a few who are not actually concerned in theft, they all know of it, and think nothing so scandalous as informing against the thieves, or even acknowledging that they know any of the guilty. This they pretend is for fear of the thieves, who never fail to revenge themselves by plundering the cattle of such as do give the least intelligence; but this is all pretence, for they know they would be protected. It is no great wonder that they are thieves, since from the earliest settlement the Camerons, McDonalds, Kennedys, McGregors, Robertsons, which are the prevailing names here, thieves have always been protected by the gentlemen of estates, who kept them to join in every rebellion, as the most desperate, the most hardy, and most proper to be made officers of, or give lesser commands to.[8]

This clearly shows that the attitude towards the natives was virtually racist. The officer who went on to become General Wolfe, Hero of Quebec, wrote to a friend of his serving at Fort Augustus in 1755:

Mr Macpherson shou'd have a couple of hundred men in his neighbourhood... with orders to massacre the whole Clan if they show the least symptom of Rebellion.[9]

Wolfe had served in the Highlands himself three years earlier. This prejudice should hardly surprise, as his reference to the Highland Regiments on the Heights of Abraham shortly before his death shows: They are hardy, intrepid, accustomed to a rough country, and make no great mischief if they fall (*supra p20*).[10]

The tribal warrior society of the Highlands had been a thorn in the side of centralising Scottish kings since the time of David I, but the explicit racism towards them was applied by all too many English to all Scots, despite the best efforts of psychopaths like Captain Caroline Scott and Captain James Fergusson of HMS *Furnace* in brutalising their fellow Scots as delineated in the *The Lyon in Mourning*. What is most significant about these situation reports, however, is what has not been told. The Highlands of Scotland, and much of the Lowlands, was under British army occupation well into the 1750s, long after Culloden.

It was in trying to track down one of the 'lads in the heather', whom I had come across in story rather than historical source documents, that I found something that paints what is a truly disturbing picture. I was following various written stories about Iain Dubh Cameron, the Serjeant Mor as he was known, when I came across a reference to an unpublished document that gives a clear picture of what transpired not just in the Highlands but throughout Scotland in the years after 1746. Serjeant Mor and his companions, like other groups of Jacobites, had taken to the hills and were using the traditional clan skills of inter-clan cattle-raiding to support themselves. This practice had been a central part of Highland society since the Iron Age and it was this perennial pastime that had helped give the Highlanders their reputation for feuding and battle. In fact, the system was such that it involved battle not war, acquisition not conquest, and such practices have been universal throughout much of human history whenever the dominant socio-economic model has been that of tribal cattle-raiding.

The unpublished document is entitled *The Cantonment Registers of the British Army 1746–53*, and currently exists in a single copy in the library of Edinburgh Castle. It details the movements and billeting of the British Army in Scotland in those years and shows that there was hardly a glen in Scotland between Argyll and Sutherland that did not have its garrison in this period, in addition to the great fortresses of Fort George, Fort William, Edinburgh, Stirling, etc. Further to these glenhead garrisons, sometimes as few as half a dozen men, there were riding patrols of dragoons, generally based in places such as Braemar and Corgarrf Castles. These larger garrisons had up to several hundred men. This network of widespread small groups of soldiers linked by mobile parties of dragoons was, according to the Government of the time, set up to stop cattle theft. This is from a document that was posted on church doors throughout Scotland in 1749:

> In order to prevent Depredations, as much as possible, this is therefore to give notice to all concerned that whenever any cattle are stolen, the owners are immediately to cause the Track to be followed, at the same time acquainting the nearest party of soldiers who have orders to give all possible assistance for the recovering of the cattle and apprehending the thieves.

> The Country People are directed to be very Cautious in giving false Alarms, to prevent the Troops being harassed unnecessarily.

> It is recommended and Expected that the Gentlemen and principal Tacksmen in the neighbourhood of each Party would meet and concert the most proper measures for

rendering this service effectual and that they would be so good as to transmit their opinion writing to the Commanding Officer that he may give the necessary Instructions to the officers under his command to take the most Effectual Measures for the publick Service.[11]

The occupation has been interpreted effectively ever since as some sort of police action against thieves. The inference is that these *caterans* (an old Gaelic word that means warrior or raider; the difference is slight) who stayed out of Culloden were merely reverting to type – being little more than savages – and were no more than the dying remnants of a way of life that was anachronistic and past its sell-by date. As we have sitreps from as late as 1755, and from the geographical extent of such garrisons, it seems that these cattle thieves were quite effective. Of course, there was much more to this than the last gasp of an ancient way of life, though there is some truth in that idea. Many of the 'lads in the heather' must have felt that they were hanging onto their traditional way of life and culture, though many of them, particularly those who had served abroad, like Serjeant Mor himself, must have been aware that the time of the Highland clans was passing, if not already gone. The need to have such a widespread military presence tells us that there was much more to this than just the need to defend Lowland cattle farmers. *The Cantonment Register* and the sitreps speak of a wholesale long-term military occupation of a considerable part of what was the United Kingdom.

Some of what little we know about Serjeant Mor gives clues as to what was actually going on. In *Ancient Animosity: The Appin Murder and the End of Scottish Rebellion* (2004) by Lee Holcombe, we find reference to the fact that Serjeant Mor, or Iain Dubh Cameron or McMaster, as he was known, went to France sometime in the late 1740s or early 1750s.[12] This seems an odd thing for a man who was no more than a cattle thief to be doing. He was probably like many of the other Scots who went back and forth to France in the period, either carrying money or intelligence to the Jacobites who had gone to France to join Charles Edward Stuart in France, or to visit his father James in Rome.

While it is true to say that after 1746 Bonnie Prince Charlie had no further interest in Scotland – though he does seem to have retained a patronising affection for the Highlanders who had helped him while he was on the run – the Scots had not lost interest in Jacobitism. Nor had many of the English, for Charles actually paid a visit, incognito, to London in 1750 to check how the land lay and to continue plotting with Jacobite sympathisers in the capital to restore his father to the British throne. But in Scotland, those like Serjeant Mor, who 'stayed out', and those tenants who paid double rents to their clan chiefs in exile, still supported the Jacobite cause. Such chiefs as Cluny Macpherson and MacDonald of Keppoch, who stayed on in Scotland for years after Culloden, were active in keeping up this support. Given Charles's disinterest in Scotland, we have to ask ourselves why this was, and why there was felt to be a need to keep Scotland so extensively garrisoned. The fact of the matter is that the Scots who rallied to Charles's standard at Glenfinnan and in the ensuing months appear to have had a particular agenda. While the idea of a major raid leading to personal acquisition must have played some part in many individual Highlander's decision to go along with the Stuart cause, this was not true of their chiefs or of the majority of the eventual Jacobite army who came from areas we nowadays consider to be Lowland. What were they fighting for? Religion undoubtedly played a considerable part, particularly for the Scottish Episcopalians, who saw the overthrow of the Stuarts in 1688 as essentially against God's will. However, it wasn't just Catholics and Episcopalians who came out in the rebellion. While the official position of the Presbyterian Church was clearly anti-

The monument at Glenfinnan

Statue of an anonymous Highlander, sculpted by James Gillespie Graham,
on top of the monument at Glenfinnan

Stuart, this was not necessarily how their congregations, or even some of their ministers, felt. While Charles himself was no longer interested in Scotland after Culloden, the evidence suggests that the Scots themselves were driven by more than loyalty to a deposed royal house. Murray Pittock made a telling point when he wrote in 2001:

> Contemporary political cartoons noted the Jacobite Rising as a threat to the Union and showed the Jacobite forces carrying Scottish national symbols, yet the nationalist dimension of Jacobitism remains an uncomfortable and neglected fact even today.[13]

The reluctance of so many of Prince Charlie's commanders to go into England is well-known, and in the occupation of so much of Scotland by the British Army, it seems the government in London were well aware of just how nationalist the Jacobites were. The hugely unpopular Union had been driven through in the face of popular opposition less than 40 years earlier, and in the overtly racist attitudes shown in so many of the situation reports we can see that the United Kingdom was in reality anything but united. The portrayal of Scots in the cartoons of English newspapers during this period was particularly nasty, and there were regular comparisons between Highlanders and such 'savage' peoples as the so-called 'Hottentots' of southern Africa.

And so the Jacobite cause continued to be a problem for the British state. Prince Charlie was actively involved in the abortive French invasion attempt of 1759. This invasion was stopped by the British naval victory at Quiberon Bay on 20 November 1759. It is generally dealt with by historians as part of the Seven Years War, with the Jacobite aspect of it ignored. Yet, this was the true end of Jacobite hopes for the restitution of the Stuarts, though plotting did continue in a desultory fashion for some time to come.

Now, the point has already been made that the role of history is to preserve social stability, and it would be asking too much for an educational establishment paid for by taxes from England to rock the boat too much. However, the whole point of being in a United Kingdom – and the legal language of the Treaty of Union does read as if the two nations concerned are equal participants in this legal and constitutional contract – was supposedly to benefit all concerned. What benefit can Scots be seen to gain from the facts of their history being suppressed? For this is the only conclusion that can be drawn. Yes the sitreps and various reports have been published in the Albemarle Papers and in the Allardyce Papers, though much of what they contain has been ignored. What has arisen over the past 250 years is a picture of the last Jacobite Rising as having been a glorious but essentially doomed adventure by a sadly anachronistic society following a charismatic young prince like the children of Hamelin followed the Pied Piper.

It is as if the Jacobite part of our history has been put into a wee box and wrapped up in a tartan bow. The truth is far more complex. For Serjeant Mor, Cluny Macpherson and James of the Glens, who was judicially murdered in 1752 for the supposed killing of Colin Campbell of Glenure, the Jacobite cause was alive and well. The constant to and fro between Scotland and France for long after the 1750s shows that the embers of Jacobitism still glowed. And what is also incontrovertible is that the British Government was well aware of the fact. The very presence of the glenhead garrisons over such a wide area well into the mid-1750s shows this. By then, of course, the remaining cohesion of the ancient clan system had effectively been broken. The process of destroying it that had started long before by the handing out of charters for lands that had been held communally by the sword for untold generations was now complete. No longer would the fear of a Highland army, composed of men raised to be warriors, assembled at a few hours notice and ready to campaign with only the arms and food they carried, worry the powers that be. Never mind that wholesale butchery, theft and rape had been perpetrated upon their own people by the British Army, no matter that a culture that had survived and flourished in the Highlands for millennia had been smashed and scattered – it was a done deal.

Much remains to be done in investigating this period further, and while the Albemarle and Allardyce papers are freely available, the papers of the Duke of Cumberland, 1740–1760, which can be found (in microform) in libraries in Michigan, Illinois, Iowa, Texas and Australia, are not to be found in any libraries in Scotland. It puts you in mind of the old joke – 'just because I am paranoid, doesn't mean they aren't out to get me!' The executions of several of the guerillas including Serjeant Mor are recorded in the *Scots Magazine* of the late 1740s and early 1750s, where the clear inference is that they were no more than thieves.

Notes

1   digital.nls.uk/print/transcriptions/lyon/vol1/index.html

2   McHardy, SA; *School of the Moon*; Birlinn; Edinburgh; 2003.

3   McHardy, SA; *School of the Moon*, p. 24; See also Burt, E; *Burt's Letters from the North of Scotland*; Birlinn; Edinburgh; 1998. p. xxxiv.

4   cranntara.org.uk/crannta.html

5   archive.org/details/historicalpaper02allagoog

6   archive.org/details/albemarlepapersookepp

7   *Glasgow Past and Present*; David Robertson & Company; Glasgow; 1884.

8   *Glasgow Past and Present*, p. 622.

9   Wilson, B; *The Life and Letters of General Wolfe*; Heinemann; London; 1909. p. 252.

10   www.gla.ac.uk/media/media_117538_en.pdf

11   *Cantonment Registers*; p. 91. These are held in the Edinburgh Castle Library.

12 Holcombe, L; *Ancient Animosity: The Appin Murder and the End of Scottish Rebellion*; Author House; Bloomington, IN; 2004. p. 279.
13 Pittock, M; *Scottish Nationality*; Palgrave; London; 2001. p. 69.

CHAPTER NINE

Thomas Muir, the Radical

THE EARLIER REFERENCE to the refusal of the Scottish media to take notice of the remarkable anniversary that occurred at the Democracy March on 12 December 1992 leads us to the consideration of another piece of our history, and to one individual in particular. The Convention of the Societies of Friends of the People was held in Edinburgh on 12–13 December 1792 and was a meeting of men from all walks of society who wanted reform of the Parliamentary process. The then Prime Minister, William Pitt had himself been calling for reform back in the early 1780s, but on becoming Prime Minister in 1783 at the remarkable age of 24, like many before and since his reformist zeal disappeared instantly. By the early 1790s, the calls for reform were coming from all over England, Ireland and Scotland, but Pitt's one-time interest in reform was further dampened by recent events on the Continent. While the idea of reform had been talked about off and on among the British establishment for a while, what was happening in France terrified them. There is no doubt that Britain was democratic in name only at this time and that the whole parliamentary system was totally corrupt. However, the French model of change, following on from the harrowing experience of losing the American colonies, ensured that the British establishment was ready to revert to its default position of resistance to all but the most minimal change.

The Convention in Edinburgh had as one of its leading lights Thomas Muir, a young lawyer from Huntershill, near Glasgow. He had already shown himself to be no respecter of the status quo and had in fact been effectively expelled from Glasgow University for political agitation. He had simply moved to Edinburgh, where he managed to graduate in law in 1787 at the age of 22. Within a few years, he had gained a reputation as a man of principle who was unafraid to take on entrenched power. Scotland at this time was under the complete control of one man – Henry Dundas, Viscount Melville – who was so powerful that he was known as Henry the Ninth. He was the British Government's man in Scotland, like so many Secretaries of State in later years, and had his hands on all the patronage of governance. The idea that he could be subjected to any kind of democratic accountability was anathema to Dundas. He, like so many of his class and time, watched what was happening in France with horror, and when the Friends of the People met in Edinburgh his immediate reaction was to see this as seditious. Never mind that the Convention made it clear from the outset that they were interested in reform and not revolution, and that they wanted to work through the parliamentary process. By daring to challenge the corruption of entrenched power, they were considered traitors by Dundas and his friends. Although the tone of the motions at the Convention was generally pretty reasonable, it has to be said that Muir himself was a Republican and was more than happy to link up with the Irish Friends of the People. His reading out of this message from them no doubt heightened the fears of Dundas:

> We rejoice that the spirit of freedom moves over the face of Scotland: that light seems to break from the chaos of her government; and that a country so respectable in her attainments in science, in arts and in arms [...] now rises to distinction, not by a calm contented secret wish for a Reform in Parliament, but by openly, actively and urgently willing it, with the unity and energy of an imbodied nation.[1]

As with all popular movements in Ireland, there was a subtext. That, of course, was nationalism, because the rule of Britain was abhorred by many Irish people, most of whom were denied their civil rights by the mere fact of being Catholic. Thus the reference to an 'imbodied nation' was politically dangerous in that it was implicitly linking the ideas of Irish and Scottish separation from England. It is also a fact that several of the Scottish Friends, some of whom were from what were considered at the time the upper reaches of society, were alarmed at Muir's wholehearted support of the Irish.

Many of the Establishment had seen the beginnings of the French Revolution as 'a good thing'. They thought that the French Ancien Régime was too blatantly corrupt and were hoping that the French people would end up with a constitutional monarchy just like they had, never mind that their system was also corrupt – it was generally accepted, amongst the Establishment and their adherents, that the British form of government was the best that there could be. Sure, Pitt and his friends had called for reform, but all that was needed was a little bit of tinkering around the edges. When the French King Louis XVI conspired with foreign powers for an invasion of France to overturn the Revolution, the result was that he was put on trial, the sentence being that he was to be executed for treason. By this time, the English support for the original aims of the Revolution had already begun to wane but this was a step too far. The King's execution was set for 27 January 1793 and on 2 January Muir was arrested at his home in Edinburgh. He was brought before the Sheriff and charged with sedition. He denied all the charges and was released on his own recognisance (i.e. he promised to appear and answer any charges made against him when called upon to do so). However, Thomas was a wee bit on the headstrong side, and although the government had shown its hand, he proceeded to head to Paris, via London, to witness what was going on for himself. He believed that the execution of the king was a political mistake, though he had no sympathy for Louis himself. This was a brave, if not stupid thing to do.

When the authorities in Edinburgh heard he had gone, they immediately accused him of absconding and issued a warrant for his arrest, stating that he was conspiring with the French on behalf of the Friends of the People. This was a downright lie. However, it soon became known to his family, who sent word to Thomas in Paris, letting him know what was going on and suggesting he head for America. Early in February, war was declared on France and soon after Muir was declared to be a fugitive. This made the idea of going to America even more sensible but that is not how things panned out. With Britain and France now at war, it was no easy matter to get back over the Channel and it wasn't until April that he was given a passport to leave France. It then took until July for him to get an American ship to Belfast. This was the *Hope*, out of Baltimore. It would have been easy to stay on board and sail on to America, but Muir disembarked at Belfast and then headed over to Stranraer. He had no intention of avoiding his day in court. He was no doubt confident that he could prove that he had not committed any crime at all. However, on landing openly at Portpatrick he was immediately arrested. While Muir might have been confident he could successfully defend himself against all charges, Dundas had other plans.

Muir's trial started on 30 August 1793. The jury had been packed with government loyalists who were in Dundas's pocket and it was obvious that Muir had no chance whatsoever. He was found guilty of sedition and sentenced to 14 years transportation to Botany Bay. After his trial came similar procedural farces as Maurice Margarot, Thomas Fysshe Palmer and Joseph Gerrald were dragged before the court, and all received the same sentence. Shortly after their trials, Thomas Skirving was also found guilty of sedition, for circulating Tom Paine's book *The Rights of Man*,[2] and was given a similar sentence. After spending sometime on a rotting prison ship in the Thames, they were put on board the ship *Surprise* and headed off to New South Wales.

The show trials they were subjected to can be seen as a reaction of the British ruling class to any idea of reform, terrified as they were that the seeds of the French Revolution might find fertile ground in Britain. A comment by Lord Braxfield at Skirving's trial makes the position very clear. Skirving said:

'But remember, my Lord, Jesus Christ was a reformer too'. 'Muckle he made o' that. He was hanget', was Braxfield's retort.[3]

No one was subjected to the same treatment in England. Was this due to the fact that the Friends of the People in Scotland were much more of 'the common sort'? The fee for membership of the Societies of Friends of the People in Scotland was pennies, while in England it was guineas. Or was it that it was just so easy to treat people so despicably in a country which was being run as a despotism? Either way, the upshot of the whole affair was that these men, who are remembered, particularly in Australia, as the Scottish Political Martyrs, were sent off on a journey from which few had ever returned. Escape from Botany Bay was considered impossible and the death toll amongst prisoners was high. In fact, two of the Martyrs did see Europe again: Margarot, who served out his sentence, and Muir, who... well, we will come to that.

Even if he had been known purely as one of the Scottish Political Martyrs, Thomas Muir would have to be seen as a remarkable man. He stood unafraid against what he saw as the forces of corruption and despotism, and surrendered his own freedom as a result. However, Thomas was not a man to accept things easily and although there is some evidence to suggest that he settled down to running his own small farm in Australia – he was a transportee, not a common criminal sentenced to hard labour – what happened next is truly remarkable.

The news of his trial and those of the others spread quickly, and reports of it were published in America. Given their relatively recent problems with entrenched British power, many Americans saw Muir as a martyr to the cause of Freedom. Even such a luminary as George Washington was said to have become personally interested in Muir's case. Some people have said that what happened next was a deliberate project to rescue Muir but this requires further investigation. What we do know is that a ship was fitted out in New York for a Pacific voyage under the command of Captain Dorr in the summer of 1795 and in January 1796, the *Otter* appeared off Botany Bay.[4] There are rumours that Burns and Muir had met back in Scotland and certainly Burns suggested in a postscript to 'Scots Wha Hae' (1793) that the song was written in honour of Muir and his friends. He wrote that he had been inspired by Bruce's 'glorious struggle for Freedom, associated with the glowing ideas of some other struggles of the same nature, not quite so ancient'. Burns was working for the Excise by the time Muir came to Edinburgh – and meeting with such an openly active Radical would not have been to Burns's advantage, but it is not too much of a stretch to see this postscript as a coded allusion to Muir.

The *Otter* landed at Botany Bay claiming to be on its way to China and by the time it left, it seems Muir had already set out to sea in a small boat he had previously bought. Out of the sight of land he boarded the Otter and headed of America. There are different versions of what happened next. A story circulated that the *Otter* was wrecked in Nootka Sound in Alaska where she had gone to hunt for seals, and that only Muir and two others survived. After living for some time with a local tribe of Native Americans, he set out south for Mexico, thousands of miles away. What actually appears to have happened is that he went up to Vancouver Island on board the *Otter*, Captain Dorr being set on trading for furs and Muir definitely came into contact with various local natives, narrowly avoiding being captured by a particularly fierce local chief. He then boarded a Spanish naval

Burns Statue, Dundee

ship *The Sutil* which was visiting the area and headed with them down to California. The west coast of what is now the USA was still under Spanish rule at the time and Muir went to stay with the Governor of California, Don Diego Borica at Monterey for a while. From here his plan was to cross Spanish America and get to Cuba where he would take a ship from Havana to the United States to meet up with George Washington. Things did not work out that way.

Although he got on well with the Governor, part of Don Diego's official duties was to report the arrival of any foreigners to the viceroy in Mexico. Muir went on *The Sutil* down to San Blas in Mexico. The Viceroy, Braciforte, took a very dim view indeed of his subordinate consorting with such a radical firebrand as Muir and had no intention of letting Muir proceed to the United States, and had him sent first to Mexico City then to Vera Cruz from where he was to be sent to Spain. First, he was sent on a warship to Havana where he spent a few months in prison. Muir had hoped there would be an American consul there whom he could contact, as he believed if the American government found out he was in jail in Cuba there was a good chance they would try to have him released and sent to the US. His luck was out however, the American consul having recently headed back home, and after his spell in jail he was loaded on the ship *Ninfa* which was heading back to Spain in convoy with another ship the *Santa Elena*. On the 26 April 1797 approaching Cadiz, the Spanish ships ran into a Royal navy patrol. Some have said that the Navy knew Muir was on board, but with the two countries now at war they needed no extra reason to attack. The ensuing battle was short. In it, Muir had half of his face blown off by a cannon ball, losing an eye in the process. Once the Spanish ships surrendered, a party of British sailors came aboard the ship where Thomas lay. Among them was an officer who had known Thomas in Edinburgh. He recognised him despite his injuries and decided that he was hurt so badly that it was only a matter of time before he died.

After the Spanish ships had been commandeered by the British, the Spaniards, along with the comatose Thomas, were put in the ship's boats to row ashore. Somebody, perhaps the officer, sent word home that the famous radical Thomas Muir had died in the battle. Only he hadn't. When the boats reached the Spanish shore, Muir was sent off to hospital in Cadiz. Slowly he recovered and it seems he then wrote to Thomas Paine, who was in Paris. It is difficult to understand how he could have known that Paine was in Paris, but relatively soon after his recovery he was allowed to leave Spain for France.[6] The two countries were allies against the British and this overrode the Mexican Viceroy's distrust.

Once he got to Paris, he was treated as a hero. For the rest of his life, Thomas was a guest of the new French government. He put forward the suggestion that an invasion of Scotland would see his countrymen rise up against the oppressive Government in London, but this seems fanciful, to put it mildly. Sadly, he was so weakened by his injury and his travels that he lived only a few years before dying in Paris without ever having seen his beloved Scotland again.

Even as just one of the Scottish Political Martyrs of the 1790s, Thomas Muir deserves an honourable place in Scotland's story as a fierce fighter for democratic rights. But his journey after leaving Britain is the stuff of a Hollywood film. He escaped from Botany Bay, which was virtually unheard of; he was nearly captured by Native Americans; he travelled the then unknown – to Europeans – West Coast of America; spent time in jails in Mexico and Cuba; survived a naval battle in which half his face was blown away; and went on to be feted as a hero in Revolutionary France. True, he did die in obscurity and no-one now knows where he was buried, but that he is so little known in his native land is yet another reflection of the sad fact that Scotland's history is still beset by problems created by the gatekeeper mentality. There are several accounts of his life, some of which are on the fanciful side,

Martyrs' Monument, Edinburgh

but he truly had a remarkable life. To this day, Thomas Muir and his companions are better known in Australia than in Scotland. In the USA, his closing speech at that farce of a trial was long taught as a classic piece of declamation:

> As for me I am careless and indifferent to my fate. I can look danger and I can look death in the face, for I am shielded by the consciousness of my own rectitude. I may be condemned to languish in the recesses of a dungeon, I may be doomed to ascend the scaffold; nothing can deprive me of the recollection of the past – nothing can destroy my inward peace of mind arising from the remembrance of having discharged my duty.[7]

The reply from the presiding judge Lord Braxfield, hand-picked by Dundas, was:

> Is the panel guilty of sedition or is he not?... Mr Muir had

gone among ignorant country people making them forget their own work, and told them that a reform was absolutely necessary for preserving their liberty, which, if it had not been for him, they would never have thought was in danger. I do not doubt that this will appear to the jury, as it does to me, to be seditious... A Government in every country should be just like a corporation, and in this country it is made up of the landed interest which alone has a right to be represented. As for the rabble who have nothing but personal property, what hold has the nation of them? What security for the payment of their taxes? They may pack up all their property on their backs, and leave the country in the twinkling of an eye, but landed property cannot be removed.[8]

Those sentiments find a dark echo in the ongoing power of the landed interest even in Scotland today...

Though Muir is a fascinating figure, the real tragedy is that so little has been taught about this period of Scotland's past. The support for the Radicals in the 1790s was widespread and other events in the period show that Scotland was anything but a free country back then. The militia riot at Tranent in August 1797, which saw 12 local people being shot down in the streets, was only one instance of widespread civil disturbance in the period as the common people resisted the drafting of young men into the army to fight the Empire's foreign wars.[9] In a move worthy of George Osborne, the government had allowed those who could afford it to pay a bounty to have their sons removed from the draft, which of course only made things worse. The raising of Fencible regiments (i.e. soldiers who were supposed only to be defending against possible invasion by the bloodthirsty French) was understood as a means of raising new troops who could be, and often were, sent any- where around the world. This followed a pattern set in the raising of Highland Regiments in the middle of the century.

This whole period of Scottish history needs greater examination and it is telling that one of the best sources for the period, *Radicals and Reformers in Late Eighteenth-Century Scotland* (1989) by Paola Bono, which is an annotated checklist of pamphlets, books and other documents of the time, was published through The Scottish Studies Centre of the Johannes Gutenburg University in Mainz, Germany.[10] That the Radicalism of this period carried on despite the corrup-

Scottish Political Martyrs' Monument, Nunhead Cemetery

tion and repression of government can be seen in the later debacle of 1820, which is generally known as the 1820 Rising.[11] Although stage-managed by government informers, the 1820 event did see thousands of workingmen march on Glasgow calling for reform. It is also interesting that one of the banners carried proclaimed 'Scotland Free or a Desert' which appears to be a reference back to the speech attributed to Calgacus before the Battle of Mons Graupius in 80CE against the invading Romans under Agricola. The awareness of Scotland's history among the common people of Scotland at that time reflects a strong commitment to the Radical ideas that had been forcefully propounded by Muir and his companions a quarter of a century earlier.

There is another memorial to the 'Scottish Martyrs' in Nunhead Cemetery in south-east London and several books have been published on them in Australia. In fact, only two of them, Muir and Skirving, were Scots, though all were tried and found guilty for activities in Scotland.

Bust of Thomas Muir by
Alexander Stoddart, on
permanent exhibition at
Bishopbriggs Library

Although this period of our history has been ignored by most of our historians, the legacy of it is quite remarkable. One of the men active in the Societies of the Friends of the People was James Wright from Dundee, who helped ensure that Thomas Paine's *The Age of Reason* was published and distributed in Scotland. He was a successful ironmonger and the story goes that, fearing arrest after the trials of Muir and the others, he rowed out to the middle of the River Tay one night and threw all his incriminating papers into the water, before returning to shore and heading off incognito to America, where he died a few years later.[12] He left two daughters behind, one of whom, Fanny, showed herself to be every bit as radical as her father.

She was something of a prodigy, having a 'philosophical romance' called *A Few Days in Athens* (1822) published when she was just 18. However, it was not as a novelist she made her name. She visited the USA in 1818 at the age of 23 and over the next few years she began to take an interest in the fight against slavery. After a trip back to Europe, she returned to America. She then set up a farm in Tennessee, manned by slaves who worked off their sale price and became free. She hoped this would be a model for other slave-owners but was sadly disappointed. Over the next few years, she became even more radical and began to tour the United States giving talks which covered a range of topics other than slavery. She talked about female emancipation and, most provocatively, argued against all religion. This provoked a great deal of apoplexy among various levels of society and she was branded at one point 'The Great Red Harlot'.[13] To this day she is well known in the USA where she is seen as a seminal figure in the development of feminism and of radical politics in general, and is seen as an important player in the development of the Democratic Party. In Scotland, she remains almost unknown. Like Muir, her brand of politics means she has effectively been written out of our history.

Notes

1   etudesecossaises.revues.org/index220.html
2   www.ushistory.org/PAINE/rights/index.htm
3   www.siliconglen.com/Scotland/11_16.html
4   Clune, F; *The Scottish Martyrs*; Angus & Robertson; Sydney; 1969. p. 101.
5   Clune, *op.cit*, p. 113.
6   Clune, *op. cit*, p. 127.
7   Mackenzie, P; *The Life and Trial of Thomas Muir Esq*; P Walsh; Rutherglen; 1919. p. 44.
8   Ibid.
9   Mullay, S; *Scotland's Forgotten Massacre*; Moorfoot; Edinburgh; 1979.
10 Bono, P; *Radicals and Reformers in Late Eighteenth-Century Scotland: An Annotated Checklist of Books, Pamphlets and Documents Printed in Scotland, 1775–1800*; Peter Lang; Frankfurt am Main; 1989.
11 www.electricscotland.com/history/1820/
12 Millar, AH; *Haunted Dundee*; Malcolm Macleod; Dundee; 1923. p. 48.
13 www.nndb.com/people/491/000206870/

Epilogue

IN THIS BOOK, I have taken a look at various periods of Scotland's past and outlined potentially different interpretations to what I have been calling Received Opinion. Many more topics could have been treated in a similar fashion as the underlying problem is one of attitude. Using the term Received Opinion to represent Establishment thinking, north and south of the border, is one way of flagging up that the problem is a deep-rooted one. And it is something that impinges directly on day-to-day life in Scotland. In the debate preceding the recent Independence Referendum in Scotland, many on-line news sites and blogs, such as Newsnet Scotland, Bella Caledonia, National Collective, Wings Over Scotland and Lallands Peat Worrier, returned to the same point, which was that the mainstream media (MSM) were united not only in their opposition to political change, but also appeared to be perfectly happy to repeat every negative story that arose about Scottish Independence. This is partly due to a tendency, most pronounced in the BBC (or should that be EBC, with E for Establishment), to pander to the metrovincial opinions of the London commentariat. Effectively in the media, as in the economy, London rules. Over the past three decades, the MSM has slithered ever deeper into a mire of celebrity-obsessed, dumbed-down mediocrity that treats its readers and viewers as idiots. Hand in hand with this goes a habit of broadcasting PR-driven pieces instead of analysis and an utterly woeful lack of incision when interviewing government spokespersons. The most blatant distortions are allowed to pass unchallenged. This, I would suggest, is part and parcel of the problems that pertain to the treatment of our history. Simply put, Scottish history and culture are seen by far too many in the media, and even yet in education, as something if not actually embarrassing, then irrelevant to them, in their shiny, metrovincial-inspired bubbles.

This pathetic pseudo-metrovincialism runs deep and in political terms means that the MSM care only for party politics as operated in the two different parliaments. The current assault on the working poor and the unemployed by the Bullingdon Bullies of Westminster is accompanied by the wholesale profitisation of the NHS, with hardly a squeak of protest from the other Westminster time-servers. In Scotland, the limitations of the SNP have been exposed by Alex Salmond's regrettable pandering to such characters as Brian Souter and Donald Trump, as a party modelled very much on Westminster lines and just as fascinated by the rich. But, whether the MSM and the gatekeepers of Scotland are aware of it or not, as the essays in this book show, I hope, the future of Scotland is not about the SNP. It is about the people of Scotland who have never lost their sense of national identity despite the juggernaut of tosh that has been hurled at us since the Union.

In his remarkable book, *The Very Bastards of Creation* (1996), the late James D Young made several good points about the historical relationship between Scotland and England. Like most of us, he was well aware of how easily the metrovincial media and their lickspittle lackeys north of the border will scream about any perceived incident of anti-Englishness. Young quoted John Wilkes, the most famous Radical Englishman of the 18th century, and a great hero to many on the left, when he wrote:

> the river Tweed was the line of demarcation between all that was noble and all that was base – south of the river was all honour, virtue, and patriotism – north of it nothing but lying, malice, meanness and slavery, Scotland is a treeless, flower-less land, formed out of the refuse of the universe, and inhab-ited by the very bastards of creation.[1]

At first I wondered if he was referring to our gatekeepers, but he meant us all. It just goes to show that history has much to tell us of how we have been seen, and still are seen by many south of Hadrian's Wall. Of course, I have already stated that I am happy to be seen as one of Jock Tamson's mongrel bastards, and care nothing for what the metrovincials think.

If future generations of Scottish children are to grow up with a decent regard for themselves and a respect for their own culture and history, we must be prepared to face up to the realities of what history has to tell us. Many Scots are happy to boast of how much we have given to the world, yet ignore our role in slavery, the brutalisation that accompanied the expansion of the Empire and within our own dynastic past a catalogue of dastardly behaviour worthy of the Borgias. By truly facing up to our history we will take control of it and be able to face the future knowing who we are. As a nation founded well over a thousand years ago, we are known and admired throughout the world. It is time that we knew ourselves better.

Note

1   Young, J.D, *The Very Bastards of Creation*; Clydeside Press; Glasgow 1996, p27

A Wish List

IT WOULD BE A bit impertinent to draw attention to what are glaring anomalies in Scottish history without suggesting some form of improvement. The topics covered in the essays herein could all, of course, do with considerable more research and elucidation, but a great deal more could be done. I have commented on the sad reality that too much energy has been expended on digging up Roman remains for far too long and I would hope that the recent increase of archaeological investigation into 1st-millennium Scotland is something that can be built on in the future. This, I would suggest, should go considerably further than investigations of Pictish and Scottish sites. We need to know much more about Galloway, Strathclyde, the Borders and the lands of the Gododdin, and archaeology would seem to be our best way forward, given the paucity of written early-source materials pertaining to these areas. Similarly, much more investigation needs to be done in the Hebrides to develop a proper stratigraphical timeline of human occupation there – from the retreat of the Ice to the arrival of the Christians and the introduction of literacy. In terms of the point that we should start a timeline of Scottish 'history', the finds at Elsrickle dating to circa 12000BCE point up that many of the base assumptions about our ancestors are fundamentally flawed. As the astounding discoveries at Ness of Brodgar continue to show, what we have been told about the past of Scotland and its people is not supported by the evidence. Similarly, if the re-interpretation of the evidence from Warren Field at Crathes is correct and a calendar was developed here in Scotland that assimilated solar and lunar reckoning, millennia before similar developments in the Middle East, we will have to factor that in, too.

There are specific sites that I find particularly interesting – the Laws of Monifieth, which has a unique long-term diversity of built artefacts, and Lochan Dubh in Strathardle, which according to local tradition may contain artefacts from the battle of Blath Bhalg in 729CE, when Pictish tribes fought there. A particular bee in my bonnet is the island of Scarba, which I believe is a place of considerable significance that needs to be studied in depth, partly because of its location on the north side of the Corryvreckan whirlpool, the third largest in the world, and partly because of its proximity to the stunning ritual landscape of Kilmartin Glen. The significance of these and other places is reflected variously in the oral traditions that have survived, and I will give just one example.

In JF Campbell's utterly seminal collection of oral tradition, *Popular Tales of the West Highlands* (1890), there is a tale called Mac Iain Direach. This has long fascinated me due to its links to the Paps of Jura and the involvement of the magical Seven Big Women of Jura, whom I have no doubt originally numbered nine. However, the part of this tale set on Jura starts, in fact, on Scarba. The place where the hero lands is named as Baigh nan Deargan and I went there several years ago. There is a cave there, Uamh na Deargan – the cave of the Little Red One – and it is obvious as soon as one goes through the natural stone arch outside it and into the cave, that it conforms to so many others in the area, in that the flat surface, and blackened rocks on one wall speak of ancient human habitation. In addition to that, however, the cave is formed where there is a clear geological rift. On one side, the rocks are tinged with red, which may have something to do with the name. Just on the fault line in the roof of the cave, there is a peculiar outcropping of rock. It is the size and shape of a baby's skull, pointing downwards and it does not take too much imagination to see this as something which would have been associated by our ancestors with the act of giving birth. Of course, there will always be those who shout 'coincidence' – it stops them having to think – but I believe that this natural outcropping combined with human occupation, possibly over a considerable time, suggests that this may well have been a place of special sanctity in the distant past.

There are many other locations scattered around Scotland where the combination of oral tradition, surviving in story and place names, and often linked to ancient monuments, suggests they are worthy of investigation. If we want to be clear about who we are, such places will provide the material to create our own story, based on what we know of our past, rather than constantly trying to fit the data to models of understanding developed elsewhere and essentially forced upon us. Many ancient sites have stories of the Cailleach in Gaelic, the Carlin in Scots, which as I suggested in *The Pagan Symbols of the Picts*, suggest some sort of belief in a goddess-type figure in the far past. To talk of a religion would be presumptuous but underlying ideas of fertility and rebirth seem probable. Further work on this could include investigation of Bodach sites and place-names, as there seems to be two separate cosmological dualities. The first is the Cailleach and Bride or Carlin and Maiden, as a Winter/Summer or Dark/ Light paradigm, and the other is the male/female symbolism of the Cailleach/Bodach.

The link between folklore and archaeology has been at the core of much of the work of Douglas Scott over the past decade, and the archaeologist Ian McHardy has done significant work on the Cailleach, specifically in association with Calanais.

In addition to archaeology, there are other things that can be done. To this day there are Gaelic manuscripts in libraries and private collections that are untranslated, and in some cases have been considered from a primarily linguistic aspect. Until these are investigated, we will not know what they can tell us. I have personal knowledge of just one collection – the papers of JF Campbell, who organised the compilation of *Popular Tales of the*

West Highlands. My Gaelic is pretty bad but even I realised as I went through the manuscripts that there was a fair amount of material in there that never made it into the four volumes that were eventually published. What of the other collections? Likewise, there are potentially many family and estate papers which could have material of significant importance as well as many local histories which contain information from local oral tradition. In this respect, the encouragement within the Curriculum for Excellence for studying local history in our schools is to be greatly welcomed.

It is also possible that local stories, told through generations within specific families, may have things to tell us. Until we give our own history and culture sufficient respect, such material will never be found. In this respect, it is at least possible that among the diaspora there are extant stories that can teach us much – for there were whole glens of Scotland cleared out in the 19th century and, as the people went, so did the stories they had been telling each other for millennia. Some such stories may yet survive where such emigrants settled as communities – we only have to ask to find out.

Recently, I came across an unrecorded chambered cairn through following clues in the landscape and local place names. There is much to be done.

How the Future can Change History: Some Examples

ALTHOUGH HISTORY IS generally presented as an account of what actually happened in the past, history itself in fact changes. I have already mentioned the case of Schliemann who discovered the ancient city of Troy by going directly against the advice of historians and archaeologists. The history that existed before Schliemann's discovery might have seemed definitive, but it had to change to take this development into account. There are many other examples of how what has been historically accepted as 'set in stone' can change, often quite dramatically and surprisingly quickly. Another example already discussed in this book is the idea that the Scots came from Ireland, an idea which I know many people are extremely reluctant to let go of, despite Campbell's investigation.

Recently there was great deal of attention in the media to the fact that the body of Richard III of England had been found. He is a monarch whose role in history has changed several times as scholarship has changed. The story presented by Shakespeare had a profound effect on subsequent history, with Richard 'Crookback' being portrayed as a monstrous creature who had the young princes, Edward and Richard, murdered in the Tower of London. In fact, as more recent history has shown, the deaths of these princes was probably commanded by Henry VII, and there is a school of thought that now sees Richard III as more of a victim than a monster.

Shakespeare does have a lot to answer for, even in Scotland.

Many popular histories in Scotland in the 19th century describe Macbeth and his wife Gruoch in terms clearly influenced by 'The Scottish Play', portraying them as murderous monsters. What history actually tells us is that Macbeth ruled generally peaceably for 17 years and he was doubtless no more brutal in his accession to power than either the real-life Duncan or Malcolm.

Something as simple as Christopher Columbus discovering America is something that has no basis in reality. Apart from the fact that he never got to mainland America, landing on various islands in the Caribbean, he wasn't the first European to cross the Atlantic. There is some evidence that the Phoenicians may have got to the Americas in prehistory, and few people now doubt that Scandinavians under the leadership of Leif Ericson not only visited the Canadian coast, but may well have settled there for a while. *The idea that someplace can only be 'discovered' when a white male visits it for the first time is utterly offensive.*

Similarly the idea that all of the indigenous peoples of North America were nomadic Stone Age tribes when the Europeans arrived has been shown to be a fiction, a convenient narrative for an expansionist society keen to deprive the natives of their land. The Anasazi peoples of the area now known as the Four Corners – the meeting point of Arizona, Colorado, New Mexico and Utah – had an urban civilisation with extensive cities in the mountains known as Pueblos and were a settled, agrarian, sophisticated society. Likewise the mound-building societies of the Mississippi also had cities when the Spaniards first arrived, and had been building colossal mound structures since the 4th Millennium BC. Primitive they were not.

In his remarkable book *The World and Africa* (1946), the African-American scholar W.E.B. Du Bois explored a range of civilisations that had existed in Africa, making the substantial point that Egypt was a country of Africans, many, if not most of them, Negroid. The fact that many of African cultures were preliterate meant that it was easy for Imperialist Europeans to deny they ever existed. The vast stone structures of the Benin culture showed them to have been a highly developed urban society in the distant past. *Similarly complicated urban structures in the Kingdom of Kush in Sudan and the city of Aksum in Ethiopia underline the reality that history, and archaeology, is always selective and that the more you know the more you can challenge accepted versions of history.*

One of the continuing misconceptions of history and prehistory has been that sacred sites involving buildings and/or stone carving could only have been created by settled, agrarian peoples (with the subtext that they were hierarchically organised, masculine-dominated cultures) has been shown to be no more than an assumption. Currently believed to be the oldest religious structure ever found Gobekli Tepe in modern Anatolia is dated to over 1,100 years ago, meaning that it predates settled farming. It consists of a complex arrangement of carved stones and comes from a time when until recently Received Opinion would suggest the people creating this remarkable site were akin to Hollywood's idea of cavemen. Things change and what has been handed down as history in many parts of the globe is becoming increasingly tenuous.

Further Reading

THE FOLLOWING BOOKS all shed different levels of light on diverse topics, underlining the reality that our history has all too often been manufactured to suit a political agenda that reflects the needs of a British, rather than a Scottish, perspective. Many more books could have been included, but this is, I hope, a start, for those looking to learn more.

* denotes available as e-text on the web.

*ALLARDYCE, J
> *Historical Papers Relating to the Jacobite Period 1699–1750*; New Spalding Club; Aberdeen; 1895. Contains information about the post-Culloden British Army occupation of the Highlands, including from the Glenhead garrisons re: 'Highland depredations' and situation reports from Glenhead garrisons.

BEWLEY, C
> *Muir of Huntershill*; Oxford University Press; Oxford; 1981. A somewhat unsympathetic and at times downright apologetic telling of Thomas Muir's story, but at least it gets most of the facts straight.

BONO, P
> *Radicals and Reformers in Late Eighteenth-Century Scotland*; Peter Lang; Frankfurt am Main; 1989. A detailed and excellent check-list of literature of and about the period. Telling that it was published furth of Scotland.

*CALLENDER, JT
> *The Political Progress of Britain; or An Impartial History of Abuses in the British Government*; Richard Folwell; Philadelphia; 1795. A critique of the British Empire from a Scottish Radical forced to flee to the USA in the 1790s. This publication ran to several editions in both Scotland and America, and is remarkable for the strength of the author's nationalist convictions, underlining the reality that the Union has never sat well with all Scots. www.archive.org

*CAMPBELL, E

'Were the Scots Irish?' in *Antiquity*, vol. 75, number 288; 2000, pp. 285–292. A seminal article exposing the utter lack of historical or archaeological support for the idea that the Scots came from Ireland c. 500 CE. www.electricscotland com/history/articles/scotsirish.html

CLUNE, F

The Scottish Martyrs; Angus & Robertson; Sydney; 1969. The story of Thomas Muir and his companions, their show trial and subsequent banishment succinctly told.

DAVIDSON, JM

Scotland for the Scots; FR Henderson; London; 1902. Davidson was a late 19th-century Radical journalist and sometime barrister who wrote extensively on the corruption of power and the distortion of history. This is his most explicitly nationalist work.

FOWLER, JM

False Foundations of British History; Whitcombe & Tombs; Melbourne; 1943. A somewhat overstated critique of the 'Celtic' history of the British Isles but well worth reading. Available through Percy Grainger Library at Melbourne University.

GLENNIE, JS

Arthurian Localities; Edmonston and Douglas; Edinburgh; 1869. The first concerted attempt to deal with the widespread, and very early, Scottish P-Celtic traditions of 'King' Arthur, drawing on the seminal work of Skene (see below).

HAMES, S (ED)

Unstated: Writers on Scottish Independence; Word Power Books; Edinburgh; 2012. A variety of takes on the topic, of uneven but occasionally striking relevance.

HENDERSON, G

The Norse Influence on Celtic Scotland; McElhose; Glasgow; 1910. A salutary reminder of the Germanic component of many aspects of indigenous Scottish culture. We should never forget that the Gal-Gael culture of the Western Isles arose from the combination of the indigenous Q-Celtic speakers and the Germanic speaking Norse settlers.

HOPE, AD

A Midsummer Eve's Dream; Oliver & Boyd; Edinburgh; 1970.

A fabulously fascinating analysis of William Dunbar's mediaeval text, *The Tretis of The Twa Marrit Wemen and the Wedo*, that investigates the survival of truly ancient belief in Scotland. Hope suggests there was a 'fairy cult' extant in the 15th century, which is very interesting in comparison with what we know of surviving pre-Christian beliefs over the years across Scotland.

JAMIESON, J

Bell the Cat or Who Destroyed the Scottish Abbeys?; Eneas Mackay; Stirling; 1902. An analysis of just how much blame can be attached to Scottish reformers in the late 16th century for the destruction of so many of Scotland's great religious foundations.

*JAMIESON, J

An etymological dictionary of the Scottish language; to which is prefixed, a dissertation on the origin of the Scottish language. New ed., carefully rev. and collated, with the entire suppl. Incorporated; Alexander Gardner; Paisley; 1887. Jamieson's ideas that Scots did not derive from the same Anglo-Friesian roots as English are out of favour in the universities, as is his belief that the Picts (or perhaps some of them) spoke an early form of Scots. Perhaps worth revisiting in the light of recent changes to our understanding of the past.

KAY, B

Scots: The Mither Tongue; Mainstream; Edinburgh; 2010. A necessary corrective to generations of guff talked about the Scots language. But there are nane sae deif as them that willnae listen. But they'll hae tae tak tent nou.

KIDD, C

Subverting Scotland's Past; Cambridge University Press; Cambridge; 1993. An examination of the development of the standard establishment history of Scotland post-Enlightenment worked to suppress any patriotic understanding of the country's past. It is good on just how the Enlightenment was active in the 'Britishisation' of Scotland's history, but perhaps does not pay enough attention to the reality that nationalism has been a recurrent theme at many levels of Scottish culture outside the corrupted Halls of Academe.

KLEIFORTH, AL and MUNRO, RJ

Scottish Invention of America, Democracy and Human Rights: A History of Liberty and Freedom from the Ancient Celts to the New

Millennium; University Press of America; Lanham, MD; 2004. An interesting take on Scotland's international importance.

LIVINGSTON, W

Vindication of the Celtic Character, or the Scotchman as he was and as he should be; Joseph Blair; Greenock; 1890. Declared as 'a working man's history of Scotland', this is of considerable interest, if a trifle too steeped in the Celtic Dawn. Many of the books he mentions as being suppressed are nowadays available on the web, if sadly not in print at accessible prices.

MCHARDY, SA

School of the Moon; Birlinn; Edinburgh; 2003. Stories from, and some analysis of, the inter-clan cattle-raiding tradition of the Highland clans, that survived from at least Iron Age times, and how this relates to the 'lads in the heather', the Jacobites who stayed out in the Highland until the mid-1750s, helping to ensure that most of Scotland remained under British Army occupation until this time.

*MATHIESON, WL

The Awakening of Scotland; a History from 1747–1797; MacLehose & Sons; Glasgow; 1910. Although he does not cover everything in the period, this is interesting on the inter-relationships between the two countries. He tells us that during the time of Lord Bute (the first post-Union Scottish-born Prime Minister in the early 1760s): 'Wilkes and other writers complained that these immigrants from the frozen north were fattening on a public revenue to which their country contributed not a fortieth part; John Bull was announced as dead — "choked by inadvertently swallowing a thistle"; ravenous Scots were assumed to be everywhere spoiling his goods'. This text is available from www.archive.org

MEIKLE, HW

Scotland and the French Revolution; MacLehose & Sons; Glasgow; 1912. Meikle links the agitation of the 1790s directly through to the Reform Acts of the 1830s, showing that Scottish Radicalism had never gone away: 'although the dread of innovation suspended the activity of the reformers for a time, the Reform Bill of 1832 was due, in part at least, to the agitation engendered 40 years before. An attempt has also been made to trace the effects of the French Revolution in other departments of the national life, chiefly social and ecclesiastical, and to describe the role assigned to Scotland in French schemes for invading the British Isles'.

MULLAY, S

Scotland's Forgotten Massacre; Moorfoot; Edinburgh; 1979. The story of the slaughter at Tranent in 1797 provoked by local resistance to the Scottish Militia Act of that year, which looked to raise troops to fight off a perceived imminent French invasion.

ROBBIE THE PICT

Attempted Murder: A Pictish Perspective on the Treaty of 1707; Scottish Exchequer Press; Pictland; 1994. This is a partisan, readable and incisive look at the founding constitutional document of the British state. (Nae written constitution? Ma bahookie). Objective it is not, but why should it be?

*ROBERTSON, D

Glasgow Past and Present; D Robertson and Company; Glasgow; 1884. Contains a collection of situation reports from British Army Highland garrisons from 1746 into the 1750s in an Appendix. They appear to have been appended to this volume simply because someone wanted them made available. www.archive.org

*ROBERTSON, FW

The Scottish Way 1746–1946; Freedom's Decline and the Truth about the Highland Clans; The Buteman; Rothesay; 1946. Published by the Scottish Secretariat, this pamphlet is succinct and has lost none of its relevance. www.scottishrepublicansocialistmovement.org/

SCOTT, D

The Watchers of the Dawn CD-ROM 2003. For more information, contact douglas.scott@btinternet.com Detailing solar and lunar alignments from ancient monuments throughout Scotland, underlining the reality that this part of the world was no cultural backwater in prehistoric times. Available through Megalithic Portal. www.megalithic.co.uk

SCOTT, D

The Clava Cairns; For the Right Reasons Community Print; Inverness; 2010. A detailed analysis of the alignments and the folklore of this major site just south of Culloden. Available through Megalithic Portal.

SCOTT, PH

1707: The Union of Scotland and England; Chambers/Saltire Society; Edinburgh; 1979. A short yet compelling work giving a welcome Scottish interpretation of this momentous event in our history that is of considerable relevance today.

*SKENE, WF

The Four Ancient Books of Wales; Edmonston & Douglas; Edinburgh; 1868. A breakthrough work of scholarship exploring the history and literature of the P-Celtic speaking peoples of Scotland who included the Britons of Strathclyde, the Gododdin of Lothian and the Picts.
www.sacred-texts.com/neu/celt/fab/index.htm

*TERRY, CS (ED)

The Albemarle Papers being the correspondence of William Anne, second earl of Albemarle, commander-in-chief in Scotland, 1746–1747. Aberdeen University; Aberdeen; 1902. Contains information on the battle against the 'Highland thieves'.

*THE TRIALS AT LARGE OF ROBERT WATT AND DAVID DOWNIE, FOR HIGH TREASON, AT THE SESSION OF OYER AND TERMINER, AT EDINBURGH;

Alexander M'Kenzie & Co; Philadelphia; 1794. This is a report of the trial of two Scotsmen under the English law process of Oyer and Terminer in Edinburgh in 1794. Downie was subsequently hung and beheaded. www.archive.org

YOUNG, JD

The Rousing of the Scottish Working Class; McGill-Queen's University Press; Montreal; 1979. A detailed and incisive account of just how Scottish history has been suppressed. Very good indeed on the Radical and nationalist agitation of the early 19th century.

YOUNG, JD

The Very Bastards of Creation; Scottish-International Radicalism: A Biographical Study, 1707–1995; Clydeside Press; Glasgow; 1996. A fascinating investigation of Scottish Radicalism from the Union to the end of the 20th century by an unsung hero of Scottish history writing. The title comes from the mouth of that famous 18th-century English Radical, John Wilkes when he said: 'Scotland is a treeless, flowerless land, formed out of the refuse of the universe, and inhabited by the very bastards of creation'.

Photo Credits

Luath Press would like to thank all the bloggers and photographers who kindly gave us permission to reproduce their photographs throughout this book and those shared their work online through Creative Commons.

P95   Reproduction of the 'Tyninghame' (1320 AD) copy of the
        Declaration of Arbroath
        Public domain, courtesy of Wikipedia

P96   Detail from 1320 Declaration of Arbroath
        © Kim Traynor, Wikimedia Commons

P99   Robert the Bruce statue, Bannockburn
        © Kim Traynor, Geograph

P104   *An Incident in the Rebellion of 1745* (1746) by David Morier
        Public domain, courtesy of Wikimedia Commons

P106   The memorial cairn at the centre of the battlefield of
        Culloden, near Inverness in Scotland
        © Nilfanion, Wikimedia Commons

P108   *Prince Charles Edward Stuart, 1720–1788. Eldest son of
        Prince James Francis Edward Stuart* (1750) by William
        Mosman
        Public domain, courtesy of Wikimedia Commons

P115   The monument at Glenfinnan
        © Flaxton, Wikimedia Commons

        Statue of an anonymous Highlander, sculpted by James
        Gillespie Graham, on top of the monument at Glenfinnan
        © Kutsa, Wikimedia Commons

P126   Statue of Robert Burns, Dundee
        © Kim Traynor, Wikimedia Commons

P129   Martyrs' Monument, Edinburgh
        © David Hayes, used with kind permission

P130   Scottish Political Martyrs' Memorial, Nunhead Cemetery
        © Paul Farmer, Geograph

P131   Bust of Thomas Muir by Alexander Stoddart, on permanent
        exhibition at Bishopbriggs Library
        © Dumgoyne, Wikimedia Commons

Some other books published by **LUATH** PRESS

A New History of the Picts

Stuart McHardy

ISBN: 978-1-906817-70-1 PBK £8.99

The Picts hold a special place in the Scottish mindset – a mysterious race of painted warriors, leaving behind imposing standing stones and not much more. Stuart McHardy challenges these long-held historical assumptions. He aims to get to the truth of who the Picts really were, and what their influence has been on Scotland's past and present.

McHardy demonstrates that rather than being some historical group of outsiders, or mysterious invaders, the Picts were in fact the indigenous people of Scotland and the most significant of our tribal ancestors. The Picts were not wiped out in battle, but gradually integrated with the Scots to form Alba. Their descendants walk our streets today.

Written and arranged in a way that is both accessible and scholarly, this is an excellent addition to the growing body of work on the Picts.

THE COURIER

On the Trail of Scotland's Myths and Legends

Stuart McHardy

ISBN: 978-1842820-49-0 PBK £7.99

A journey into Scotland's past through the awe-inspiring stories that were at the heart our ancestors' traditions and beliefs.

As *On the Trail of Scotland's Myths and Legends* unfolds, mythical animals, supernatural beings, heroes, giants and goddesses come alive and walk Scotland's rich landscape as they did in the time of the Scots, Gaelic and Norse speakers of the past.

Visiting over 170 sites across Scotland, Stuart McHardy traces the lore of our ancestors, connecting ancient beliefs with traditions still alive today. Presenting a new picture of who the Scots are and where they have come from, this book provides an insight into a unique tradition of myth, legend and folklore that has marked the language and landscape of Scotland.

This remains an entertaining record of the extent to which history is memorialised in the landscape.

THE SCOTSMAN

Details of these and other books published by Luath Press can be found at: **www.luath.co.uk**

Luath Press Limited
committed to publishing well written books worth reading

LUATH PRESS takes its name from Robert Burns, whose little collie Luath (*Gael.*, swift or nimble) tripped up Jean Armour at a wedding and gave him the chance to speak to the woman who was to be his wife and the abiding love of his life. Burns called one of 'The Twa Dogs' Luath after Cuchullin's hunting dog in Ossian's *Fingal*. Luath Press was established in 1981 in the heart of Burns country, and now resides a few steps up the road from Burns' first lodgings on Edinburgh's Royal Mile. Luath offers you distinctive writing with a hint of unexpected pleasures.

Most bookshops in the UK, the US, Canada, Australia, New Zealand and parts of Europe either carry our books in stock or can order them for you. To order direct from us, please send a £sterling cheque, postal order, international money order or your credit card details (number, address of cardholder and expiry date) to us at the address below. Please add post and packing as follows: UK – £1.00 per delivery address; overseas surface mail – £2.50 per delivery address; overseas airmail – £3.50 for the first book to each delivery address, plus £1.00 for each additional book by airmail to the same address. If your order is a gift, we will happily enclose your card or message at no extra charge.

Luath Press Limited
543/2 Castlehill
The Royal Mile
Edinburgh EH1 2ND
Scotland
Telephone: 0131 225 4326 (24 hours)
email: sales@luath.co.uk
Website: www.luath.co.uk